THE POWER BOOK

THE POWER BOOK

200 WAYS TO MAKE POWER WORK FOR YOU!

ROSE HERCEG

JAICO PUBLISHING HOUSE

Ahmedabad Bangalore Bhopal Bhubaneswar Chennai
Delhi Hyderabad Kolkata Lucknow Mumbai

Published by Jaico Publishing House
A-2 Jash Chambers, 7-A Sir Phirozshah Mehta Road
Fort, Mumbai - 400 001
jaicopub@jaicobooks.com
www.jaicobooks.com

Published in arrangement with
Allen & Unwin Pty Ltd
Sydney, Australia, 2013

THE POWER BOOK
ISBN 978-81-8495-626-9

First Jaico Impression: 2014
Second Jaico Impression: 2016

Printed by
Nutech Print Services-India
B-25/3, Okhla Industrial Area, Phase-II
New Delhi - 110 020

CONTENTS

INTRODUCTION
THE ART OF POWER

Power is everything and nothing: awful and brilliant; obsessive and carefree; evil and dignified. Breathtaking when applied nobly; the worst of our humanity when used as a torture technique—mental waterboarding when used to lord it over someone.

This book will explore the good kind of power. The kind that garners respect. The bad kind does pretty well on its own and doesn't need any help from me.

There are two big parts to most of our lives: work and the time left over, which I will generously call play. Power and influence feature prominently in both of them, and a little help in both areas can make life somewhat easier to live. Power Plays are the tactics we use to get the things we want. And the best Power Players do this with panache and style. Some of these Power Plays are purely work-related, some sit in the wider world and some—well, I just don't know where they fit, but they're good and useful.

For quite some time now I've been stockpiling stories from work and play and life and love that have at their core the theme of power. These stories have captured my unwavering interest because they start to add up to a new way of 'doing power': less carbs, more protein. Or to put it another way, less Marilyn, more Jackie.

This book is not linear, so you can dip into it for inspiration whenever and wherever you like. It might give you a little cheat sheet on the type of power and influence that can add years to your life, because it becomes fifty percent easier to live in the world. Stuff shouldn't be as hard as it turns out being for most of us and the access-all-areas backstage pass to power is like working out the perfect haircut, one that makes you look ten times better and transforms your personality because you know you've found 'your' hair.

Wherever I can I'll recount these stories as well as why they struck me as a new way of doing power. I've tested a lot of the Power Plays and, like most things in life, it comes down to the user.

We all think we know what power should look like so we follow the same old crazy rules about it that should have been buried with shoulder pads and braces. Rules that tell us if we want to be powerful we need to be dictatorial. Or cruel. Or arrogant.

Despots and freaks usually hijack power. It feels about time to take it back. Let's restore some dignity to power and influence and relearn how to feel good about using it in the first place.

200 POWER PLAYS

ZIP IT

POWER PLAY FOR WORK AND PLAY

Of all the Power Plays I've seen and heard, this one is my absolute favourite.

There's an old Spanish proverb: 'Don't speak unless you can improve upon the silence.' Most people in business are afraid of silence but the most important skill you can ever learn is to keep your mouth shut. Get used to saying nothing and use silence to make the other guy speak. Not sure which way the wind is blowing? Don't speak until you find out. If you have nothing to say, say nothing. Shake hands with uncomfortable silence—if it doesn't make you feel like squirming in your own juices, you win. Silence can make you own a room. Silence can give you all the power. It ain't over until the fat lady keeps her mouth shut and makes the other guy sing.

▶ THE STORY

My all-time favourite Power Player is a fella who speaks very, very little. He is the classic man of few words but they're always the right ones. I'm in a meeting with him, and one of his guys is grappling with a decision and looking for direction from the Power Player. Anyone else would step in and start talking fast and loose—not this fella. He lets his guy talk himself into the decision, out of the decision, around the decision, figure out why the decision he needs to make is bothering him so much. And after all this talk, the guy works it out all on his own while the Power Player hasn't said a word. Not one. And the guy who's paced a hole in the carpet finally makes a smart (and right) decision all on his own and turns to the Power Player and says: 'Thank you—that was really hard and you made it easy.' Not one word from the Power Player. Just a nod and a reassuring smile.

WEAR YOUR POWER LIGHTLY

POWER PLAY FOR EVERYWHERE

Great leaders (and Power Players) wear their power lightly. They *never* throw their weight around. They never suffer from that type of business low self-esteem where they need to let everybody know their place in the room. Big enchiladas don't need to advertise their power. They are benevolent with their power and make space for others, and by treading gently they cultivate even more power. Power is always sexier when it's not obvious, implied rather than stated, gentle rather than bold. And it often turns out that light power-wearers tend to be much smarter (and nicer) too. Putting people at ease (especially the newbies in an organisation) usually allows for their best talents to come to the fore.

▶ THE STORY

I was once (and only once) in a meeting with a god of media. Perhaps *the* god. He waltzed into where everyone was waiting for him to hold court, and in my total terror (and awe—he looked much better in person) I knocked over my glass of water. It spilt everywhere and as I was looking for a trapdoor through which I could fall, the God of Media grabbed a pile of serviettes and started mopping up the mess. He then walked over to the water jug, refilled my glass and whispered in my ear, 'Don't worry about it, kid. If it wasn't you, it would have been me.' I've seen a lot of power in my time but nothing compares to that. Talk about wearing one's power lightly. It made the room want to walk through fire for him. Having known him for thirty seconds, I would have lain down in front of a bus.

NEVER BE A CHEAPSKATE

POWER PLAY FOR EVERYWHERE

Carry cash in your pockets at all times. Meeting for a coffee with a colleague, client or worker bee? Then you pay. And don't put a three-dollar coffee on an expense account—it makes you look cheap and small. No one with any class ever let the other guy pay, especially someone who makes a lot less money. The best advice I ever got? Cheapness travels. Cheap in the pocket? Probably cheap of character too. Generosity seems to be a dying art, but if you do pick up the bill for someone you work with, don't lord it over them. It's not a favour to be repaid, it's a courtesy you've extended, no quid pro quo. Have a more relaxed attitude to money: holding onto it too tightly is a bad habit and not picking up the tab for the odd incidental expense is poor form.

▶ THE STORY

On my first day in a company a man came over to introduce himself, but mainly to put me in my place and let me know who was boss. After our little 'chat' he asked if I wanted a coffee and, thinking it would be polite to say yes, I said, 'Only if you're getting yourself one.' Five minutes later he walked into my office with a big smile. Handing over the coffee he said, 'That's three dollars fifty.' Back then I was filled with too much smart-arse (in which I now take absolutely no pride) so I handed him a twenty-dollar note and said, 'Keep it, and the next time you go you can take it off the balance.' Now, my behaviour was totally out of line and nothing at all excuses it, but his was perhaps the cheapest moment I have ever witnessed in my life. So don't be cheap. Like cheap aftershave, it will stay behind way after you have left the room. This story happened a dozen years ago and I remember every second of it—always have, always will.

TAKE A BREATH

POWER PLAY FOR EVERYWHERE

This one takes practice because breathing is a lost art: powerful people always remember to take a breath. They stop before they blurt it out and learn to take that beat in a conversation. Sounds strange but when you think about it, it's not. Taking that breath is powerful because you become aware of what could come out of your mouth and give it a chance to bounce around in your head before it hits the room. Your audience will learn that if you speak, it's worth listening to. And when people sit up and listen, that's when power becomes influence. This type of influence is considered, thoughtful and, ultimately, very cool.

▶ THE STORY

A woman I bow down to, both for her wit and her style, was in a meeting where I would have set the building on fire if it had been me. An idiot sitting opposite baited her by saying that women are 'too emotional' in business and that's why they 'never get to the top'. This Power Player took a breath, at least five seconds' worth (which is a long time when you count them out in your head). The entire room was holding its collective breath. Her answer? 'I get paid for my talent, my intellect and sometimes even my emotion. If you had more of what I have, then you'd be my boss and not the other way around.' The response was measured, merciful and spot-on, all because she'd taken a breath and gathered her wits without launching a venomous attack on a misogynist.

STOP NEEDING TO BE RIGHT

POWER PLAY FOR EVERYWHERE

Truly powerful people don't put a lot of stock in always being right. They put much more stock in being interesting and original. Powerful types also know that fresh is the currency of business today. Don't misunderstand. Powerful types do seem to have a knack for being right when it counts, but they figured out early on in their careers that right doesn't get you noticed or promoted. It's expected. What does get you noticed is a brain that can deliver original and unusual, nuanced and nimble. If you can let go of needing to be right all the time, you can start focusing on being interesting. So few people are—dull, unimaginative, sober and generic seems to be the colour of the boardroom these days. Originality (even if it ends up being the wrong strategy) equals power, and that's the type of Power Play few people can pull off. Learn how to and you can rule the world.

▶ THE STORY

A Power Player I worship made a spectacularly incorrect recommendation. His idea was brilliant—fresh, original and thrilling—but it was the wrong way to go. He didn't factor in some financial information (which he should have researched) and this news would have cancelled out the validity of the idea. Regardless, I remember thinking that his brain was unbelievably good and the client saying exactly the same thing too. He may have been wrong but his ideas meant that respect and esteem for him grew tenfold.

DON'T MATCH A COMPLIMENT

POWER PLAY FOR EVERYWHERE

When it comes to compliments, powerful types know how to accept one. More importantly, they don't fall for the mistake of immediately returning one. At best, it comes off as disingenuous; at worst, a defence mechanism employed to deflect praise and make the recipient of said compliment look humble (when they're likely not). It's a little bit pathetic and shows the recipient of the compliment to be unsure of his or her own talent. Influential types ensure a compliment they give is separate to one they receive. This means that when they do give a compliment, the receiver of this compliment knows it to be real and heartfelt. True power is praising someone honestly and giving a compliment when it is most warranted, and not as a deflective device or 'good manners'. Because there ain't a lot of power in that.

▶ THE STORY

Someone once gave me compliment on what I was wearing. It was a great dress: vintage Dior that women lucky enough to work used to wear to the office in the fifties. The minute it was given I immediately returned the compliment, even though the guy was wearing the worst suit I have ever seen. He had a fading black eye and tomato sauce (or blood) on his tie and lapel. By saying something nice to him, all I did was have every set of eyes in the room staring at his suit and its stains, the black eye and comb-over. If a five-year-old had been in the room, even they would have thought I was being deliberately cruel. I wasn't, but it didn't matter—sometimes it doesn't matter what it is, it matters what it looks like. If it's not true, don't do it. Not ever. Not to feel gracious, not to fill the space in the room. It never works and you end up looking mean, just like I did.

BE FUNNY, BE FEISTY—KNOCK IT DOWN WITH HUMOUR

POWER PLAY FOR WORK

Powerful people know that humour is the greatest weapon in any boardroom. Someone comes at you with serious and stern? Return the remark with a big dose of funny. Never forget to bring a laugh into any tense room. The most influential people use humour to charm and disarm. They understand that a dose of humour can lighten the load and return some equilibrium to a very testy situation. I'm not talking about goofy or inappropriate stuff, just a well-placed phrase delivered at the right moment. Humour is the best defence in any situation, nothing else comes close. It will put the pin back in any grenade, blunt the pen of any vicious hack and soften the tongue of any malicious gossip.

▶ THE STORY

I was in a meeting watching a guy searching for the words to tell his boss that his team had made a huge mistake on a piece of business and they'd have to pay serious dough for the mistake themselves. As the young man searched for the words, clearly terrified, the CEO said, 'Are you trying to ask me out on a date? You know I'm married, right?' The room laughed loudly and the young guy came clean about the problem (easily and calmly), and then the room could focus on how to fix it. The CEO used humour in the best way possible. Not only was it a gracious thing to do (shit happens in business) but the love and respect in the room for that CEO was palpable. The truly powerful understand the real power of funny.

BE MERCIFUL

POWER PLAY FOR EVERYWHERE

It was true in the New Testament and it's true today: the powerful are merciful when most of us would choose to be vindictive. Someone screws up and our first instinct is to stick their head on a piñata and kick the crap out of them. That's taking the low road. The powerful grow their influence by showing mercy. Rather than flog the guy who made the boo-boo, they know that this is a complete waste of time, and some pretty low-rent behaviour too. What's required is mercy. That's what we call the high road. Once emotions have settled down, powerful types can then decide what action needs to be taken regarding the one who screwed up—maybe drastic action, maybe nothing. Either way, mercy and compassion are characteristics of the truly powerful. They remember to walk a mile in other people's shoes and that everyone is entitled to a mistake or two. Fixing it is what matters.

▶ THE STORY

I made the most monumental screw-up you can make. Shame and humiliation stops me from writing the exact words I wrote on the card, but suffice to say I incorrectly sent flowers to a client's family because we'd heard his wife had died. No one's wife had died—she'd dyed her hair pink for a charity. The client (a very superstitious type) went nuts, understandably. My boss should have kicked my arse to the corner but he did not. He was merciful and told me one thing and one thing only: 'Don't do it again.' That was it. Not only exceptionally merciful but all class too.

MYSTERY IS GOOD

POWER PLAY FOR EVERYWHERE

Power Players know when to share and when to hold something back. Get out of the habit of telling people your story—they don't need to know. In fact, people need to know a lot less than you think. We live in an age where we think disclosure and sharing is good, but those who hold power and influence know it's not. A little mystery is alluring and, frankly, the charm of a person often lies in the unknown. It's the same in business as it is in a relationship: people don't need to know everything about you. Hopefully you're noticing a theme here. Less talk. More silence. A little mystery. It all adds up to a lot more power—not the malevolent kind, the attractive kind.

▶ THE STORY

This story still knocks me out every time I think of it. I met a guy a few years ago when I was living in New York who had this air of mystery about him; a wonderful presence. I watched him all night as he walked from group to group demonstrating his world's greatest listening skills. Every time somebody got close to asking him his story, he gently and shrewdly changed the subject. I guarantee that everyone went home that night wondering who this terrific, smart, funny, handsome guy was. About a year later I found out that he was a Secret Service agent on the president's detail. Yet when conversation turned to politics and snide comments were made about his boss, he'd said absolutely nothing. Sometimes it serves you better if people know nothing about you. Keep some things to yourself. It's very, very attractive.

⬆ KNOW YOUR DEAL BREAKERS

POWER PLAY FOR EVERYWHERE

Business (and relationships) has a strange way of moving your personal line—the imaginary one you draw in your head about what you're willing to do. True power knows when to walk away. To be powerful, you can never move that line. In business, the powerful know that any power they have will be quickly obliterated if they trade in their principles for some dough. In life, the powerful know that there are things they cannot turn a blind eye to. Get to know your line. Fall in love with it, marry it and never divorce it. It can be very useful in business knowing what your deal breakers are. Doing so means you've made some firm decisions, and there's a nice feeling of comfort in that. The truly powerful and influential know that real power comes from knowing when to say no.

▶ THE STORY

A very long time ago I dated a guy who, when I think of it sanely and calmly, was an awful man. He was great looking but a bad guy: mean, competitive, without conscience or integrity. And every time he said something demeaning, I'd make excuses for it, blame his terrible upbringing or his abusive mother. But if I'd taken a good look at my deal breakers I'd have known that every single one of those character traits was over my line. I could have saved myself a lot of heartache and drama. I cried a river over a guy who wasn't worthy to lick my shoes. Know your deal breakers because it will save you.

BE IMAGINATIVE

POWER PLAY FOR EVERYWHERE, BUT ESPECIALLY AT WORK

Every Power Player knows that imagination is gold. If you don't have one, get one, and fast. Imagination can dig you out of a hole. It can dazzle your team. And, most importantly, it tells the world that you are able to conjure up out of absolutely nothing something magical and brilliant. Imaginative Power Players have a talent that they can turn on anytime, anywhere, and they know that no one can dispute a genius idea when they hear one. Mostly, though, they have genuine faith in being able to call on their talent when it's required. Like a superhero who knows his power will never fail him, they know that their imaginative streak will always be there to deliver. They know their imagination can get cynical corporate types to feel like they are eight years old all over again. And transporting an ageing, fat, tired dude back to his childhood is real, hard-to-come-by power.

▶ NO STORY . . .

Because imagination is inspiration, and on this one you're on your own.

BE PATIENT

POWER PLAY FOR LIFE

Sounds easy. Turns out it's very hard. Patience these days seems to have very little place in a world of instant everything. People start getting antsy if the elevator doors close slightly slower than warp speed, so there's no telling what will happen when someone takes a little longer than necessary to make their point in a meeting. Power Players never tap their foot. They don't sigh loudly when someone is taking their time placing a food order and they *never* look disapproving when someone says they need more time to make up their mind on a big decision. Power Players worked out pretty early in the piece that patience is an incredibly beautiful human quality. And when you're patient with your colleagues they make far fewer mistakes, their responses are more thoughtful, and they feel they can relax in their working environment. True power is being able to sit there and wait quietly, trusting that the person in question will make it in their own time.

▶ THE STORY

As a little kid I remember my dad waiting for me to tie up my shoelace. It must have taken me close to twenty minutes but he stood there patiently and waited. It occurred to me many years later that almost every other dad would have taken over the shoe-tying in exasperation (and to speed up proceedings). Not my dad. People talk about patience being a virtue but very few of us really get what that means. I don't know if you can learn patience but try this: let a four-year-old choose their own clothes for the day and let them get dressed all by themselves. That's patience. If you can incorporate real patience into every facet of your life, you will always be the most powerful person in the room.

TALK ABOUT THEM INSTEAD OF YOU

POWER PLAY FOR LIFE

The truly influential always, always get people to open up about themselves. There's an incredible power in getting others to tell you their stories. Truth is, most people love answering questions about themselves, especially when the questions are smart, warm and heartfelt. Power Players get the power of having people bare their soul and tell the truth. But here's a word of caution to all you power seekers: having this skill (and the knowledge you'll garner from it) is an honour, so don't screw around with this information. Respect it. Keep it safe. Don't use it to mess with someone's head—that crap belongs in all those dumb books about malevolent power. If you're after that stuff, stop reading right now. You won't find any here.

▶ THE STORY

My friend's dad came over to dinner and my friend bet me fifty dollars that I couldn't get his dad to talk about himself. Six hours later, the dad was telling the entire dinner table about his relationship with his mother, how he learned to love his wife, what he was most afraid of . . . What most of us want is to be heard, and most people don't speak not because they don't want to but because nobody ever bothers to ask they how they feel and what they think. Letting somebody talk (and I mean really talk) is an incredibly powerful move. You'll be amazed at how rarely it happens and how much people appreciate the chance to speak.

GET BEHIND OTHER PEOPLE'S IDEAS

POWER PLAY FOR WORK

Power Players get behind other people's good ideas. If you hear a good idea from someone, use your power to help make it real. There are few things that will build your influence more than lending weight to an idea whose time has come and doing whatever is required to bring it to life. It's a noble use of power when you help other people realise their dreams. It's cool and it's classy and it's the stuff of folklore when you put your own idea to one side to get behind a much better one. Be magnanimous. Be grand. Be just. If you gain a reputation for getting behind other people's ideas, you will also be the most powerful person in the room.

▶ THE STORY

I sat in a big honcho meeting with the head of a magazine publishing company. It was the early days of the internet and the CEO was bemoaning the problem of protecting their copyright. The nineteen-year-old trainee in his first month at the company spoke up. He said that in this age of digital content, the magazine company should consider promoting the sending and sharing of content instead of trying to stop it, given that it would happen anyway. The kid's boss, a mean man in a bad suit and cheap shoes, scowled at him for speaking up. But the CEO paused to look the kid in the eye and said, 'That's a bloody great idea, Tim.' The CEO honcho then made sure that every editor, writer and publisher of each of his magazines used every conceivable opportunity to promote the sharing of their content. Turns out this tactic breathed new life into their publications and increased their newsstand sales considerably. The CEO let everyone know that the idea belonged to the kid. And the man with the cheap shoes? Fired for stealing six thousand dollars' worth of office supplies. The kid? Today he's general manager of a pay TV channel.

GET STRAIGHT TO THE POINT

POWER PLAY TO SURVIVE THIS WORLD

The powerful have an especially gentle way of delivering bad news. Knowing how to get straight to the point, with tact and without cruelty, is one of the very best lessons you can ever learn if you hope to be an all-star in the power stakes. Getting straight to the point can often be confused with bluntness: don't make that mistake because that's not what this is about. It's about telling the truth in the most compassionate way possible. No one enjoys small talk when there's something on the table that needs to be discussed. And no one went wrong by ditching the fluffy and moving on to the important stuff. It's also a sign of great respect to tell the straight story with courage and not waste people's time.

▶ THE STORY

I once overheard my boss firing someone in his team. I can't remember his exact words but it went something like this: 'Jack. You're talented. You're fun to work with and you're a good guy. You're also fired. It's awful. It's not fair. In fact, it sucks. But we've lost the account and next week we lose two more. Of course, I'll give you a great reference but as of next Friday, you don't work here any more. I'm sorry. If there is anything I can do, let me know and it's done.' I always thought it was the most benevolent speech I'd ever heard. Straight to the point, yet merciful. Jack told me later that he loved that the boss had treated him like an equal, told him straight up. No bullshit excuses, no touchy-feely crap, no weakling talk of 'realigning our strategic priorities'. Simply the facts, with an offer of real help.

NEVER, EVER BE LATE

POWER PLAY FOR EVERY SINGLE DAY

Yes, it's obvious that you should never be late. It might even be boring but it's very important. Why is it so important? Because being late and keeping others waiting is a terrible, mean and abusive power tactic. You're telling those you've kept waiting that your time is more important than theirs. I don't care if you're the Pope, you don't keep your audience waiting. The best way to show those around you that you respect them is by turning up on time. Etch this one on your forehead: never be late. Those with real, undeniable power never are.

▶ THE STORY

I once went to meet a big man who is the owner and figurehead of a global brand company. Just starting out in my career, I was terrified so I sought only fifteen minutes of his time. He turned up exactly on time and talked to me about my proposition for a little over two hours. Of the many people I've met doing business, I have never forgotten his respect for the clock, for my time, and for my ideas.

DON'T EVEN THINK ABOUT BREAKING A CONFIDENCE

POWER PLAY TO TATTOO ON YOUR WRIST

Power Players know how to keep a secret. Even if the urge hits you to tell, do not succumb. You might think that the person to whom you are imparting the juicy news is a close friend or a trusted colleague, but all you're doing is telling a tale that should have remained untold. Power Players often know lots of stuff that other people don't know. What keeps them powerful is resisting the urge to share this information. I've heard some of the most sordid, horrible, incredible (and often deadly accurate) gossip. But it stays in my head, which is where it belongs. Trust is the only remaining commodity in business so don't bend the concept as it doesn't bounce back. Once broken, it's over. So if someone tells you something and asks you not to repeat it, don't. Not once, not even a little. Real power is always resisting the urge to tell.

▶ THE STORY

I've known the worst thing there is to know about a person and I've wished I didn't. He'd exploited me on occasion and as much as I've wanted to yell his terrible secret to everyone (which would surely have cost him his job, girlfriend and every friend he'd ever cultivated), I haven't. I'm not noble or saintly, but I did give him my word, though I also suspect karma will take care of him soon enough. It's about me, not him, because if you break a confidence it's your failing. If you feel like playing the revenge card, it means you're the bad guy, not the other person. There are days where I've come close. But if I spill, I'll destroy someone's life because I want to see the show. And if I want to see a show, all I need to do is buy a ticket to the movies.

⬆ KNOW WHEN TO WALK AWAY

POWER PLAY FOR SURVIVING YOUR JOB

For most of us, it's hard to walk away, especially when you've worked on something for a long time. But sometimes walking away is the only smart, decent and prudent move. Knowing *when* to walk away is one thing; doing it quietly and with class is the clincher. Power Players know that it's time to walk when it feels like you're pushing molasses up a sandy hill—write that line on your wall. Listen to your intuition, make friends with your gut and know when to walk away. Do it quickly. Do it quietly. Do it with class.

▶ THE STORY

I was once part of a team working on a major sporting event bid. We were asked to produce a film from perhaps the most awful script we'd ever read. Against all the competition of some of the country's most powerful players, we said no. Why? Because you always have to know when to walk. We were decisive. We were fair. We were humble. We never said it was a terrible script—we simply said that it would be best produced by the writers themselves as they were closest to the material. Walking away saved us in the end because no matter the decision by the sporting body, we'd still have a full set of teeth the next day.

HAVE THE GUTS TO SAY WHAT MUST BE SAID

POWER PLAY FOR THE TOUGHEST OFFICE ENVIRONMENT

Power Players never shy away from saying what must be said. They don't obfuscate or run and hide. They don't bury their message in the fourth bullet point on a PowerPoint slide. They stand up and ruthlessly articulate what must be said no matter how uncomfortable. Why? Because real influencers are incapable of the bull it takes to pretend there's no problem. We've all been in a room full of people where everything else is on the agenda except the one thing the entire room should be talking about. The minute you say the words that everyone is waiting to hear, you elevate yourself above the fray and become the most powerful person in the room. It's glorious to watch someone tell the truth and even more so when they do it with subtlety and grace. For some strange reason it's easy for people to confuse truthfulness with bluntness. It never needs to be that way.

▶ THE STORY

On the eve of a pitch for a $200 million advertising account for an international airline, I was in a room with perhaps the greatest natural leader (and Power Player) I've ever known. The entire room was looking in anticipation to the creative geniuses whose job it was to come up with the concepts. They presented their work and the room started offering up lukewarm praise. The Power Player turned to these highly paid geniuses and said, 'Boys, this work is bad. Not only is it off brief but my Aunt Agnes could come up with a better idea and she's been dead ten years. Go back to your office, hunker down and come up with the brilliance I know you can deliver because you have done it many times before.' I loved listening to her in that room: decisive, gutsy, kind, honest and, above all, correct. She had guts, and I learned a valuable Power Player lesson I've never forgotten.

SPEAK UP IN THE MEETING, NOT AFTER IT

POWER PLAY FOR WORK

The truly influential in this world always say what they have to say then and there. Not before the meeting, not after it. Power Players stay away from those insidious corridor chats that look all buddy-buddy but deliver a grenade wrapped in silk. If they have an issue or a problem, they spell it out once and precisely in a room where everyone is present. Gossip has a strange way of becoming fact when it's repeated many times. The Power Player limits the gossip by limiting the amount of information that she or he distributes outside the official channels. It's a gutsy move by any Power Player because it says that the place to voice opinions or concerns is when everyone is present, not behind someone's back and not when someone is boozed up with tequila.

▶ THE STORY

I was in a tense meeting and a Player I adore took us through a controversial decision that head office had made. Everyone started to squirm and whisper, and the guy I adore did something rare. He told everybody that they had ten minutes to complain and moan and rant. He told them to turn to the person next to them, and protest to their heart's content. After ten minutes he called the room to order and said, 'When we walk out of this room, we speak as one voice. The decision has been made and not a single one of us will complain about it beyond these doors. Not to other staff members, not to our clients, not to the press. Not one word. We leave every malicious and destructive thought in this room.' I always thought that was one of the best ways to let people vent before asking them to leave the toxic vibe behind.

REPLACE SYMPATHY WITH EMPATHY

POWER PLAY FOR EVERY DAY OF YOUR LIFE

Power Players don't sympathise—they empathise. Pity is never sexy. Understanding someone's POV is. Empathy is as close to real as you can be because it means you've tried as hard as you can to really feel someone else's trials or tribulations. You've not dismissed them by feeling sorry for them but you've genuinely tried to see it their way. True influencers never assume they know—they know they *don't* know, and they then decide to find out what they don't know via any intel or information that can help them to empathise. In the end, most Power Players know that all the research in the world is a weak substitution for walking a mile in someone else's shoes.

▶ THE STORY

I once worked with a terrific Power Player who decided to do some volunteer work with a paraplegic group he had supported by way of an annual donation. It struck him how little he really knew about the people he had been supporting for nearly a decade, and he was ashamed to admit that the money was a type of a buffer from truly understanding their situation. He figured the only way he could understand was to get around in a wheelchair for a week. So that's exactly what he did. He got how unbelievably hard it is to be disabled in a world set up for the able-bodied. He stopped giving advice along the lines of 'the glass is half full' and 'keep a positive attitude'. It's not always a helpful stance and can dismiss the gravity and dimension of a situation that is complicated and nuanced.

↑ SAY HELLO PROPERLY!

POWER PLAY ETERNAL

You'd be amazed at how bad people are at saying hello. I mean properly. Not some sucky attempt, but a straight-up look you in the eye, shake your hand firmly (without trying to break it) hello. A warm greeting that says: welcome, you're in safe company, be yourself, we'll do whatever we can to make you feel at home. Power Players who are comfortable in their own skin go out of their way to make people feel welcome. The word 'hello', spoken with confidence and warmth, can make such a difference.

► A STORY

You're kidding, right?

REPLACE LISTENING WITH HEARING

POWER PLAY FOR EVERYWHERE

I'd swear that Power Players are born with much better hearing skills than the rest of us. They have an uncanny ability to hear not only with their ears but also with their eyes. The way they hear can calm down even the most distressed person, because when people feel truly heard, they feel understood. Appreciated. Respected. When you know that you are truly heard it immediately takes away that feeling of loneliness and isolation. A lot of us walk around every day feeling misunderstood. We speak, but all we see in return is a lot of vacant nodding, that glazed look where you know that the person you're talking to has heard nothing you've said and their mind is occupied by tonight's shopping list. This doesn't do anybody any good.

▶ THE STORY

A woman I worked with was a blubbering mess after a bad break-up. Her boss held her hand while she told her sad story. He let her continue blubbering and then said this: 'Your heart is broken and you need to be away from work. Grab your things, go home and we'll take care of stuff here. If you need anything, let me know. It's going to be okay, you'll see. I've had my heart broken too and there's nothing I can say right now that will make you better. You have to feel it and cry a lot.' The boss really heard her and didn't try to dismiss it as some terribly embarrassing personal mess she should be ashamed about. He did more than just listen, he heard.

REALLY GET TO KNOW HUMAN NATURE

POWER PLAY FOR WORK

The very best Power Players are always in the business of studying human nature. They've worked out the ebbs and flows of creativity and how to recognise the signs of fatigue and frustration. They know when someone is about to implode or, more dramatically, explode. Rather than complain about people's shortcomings, they find a way to bring out their very best. They don't react to bad behaviour but simply let it ride, altering their own behaviour so as to rebalance the person having a bad day—which is usually all it really is. People respond well to people who can handle their bad days and, in turn, they often take a moment to pause and examine their own behaviour. So be the guy who gives an inch and you'll more than likely get a mile in return.

▸ THE STORY

One of my own Power Player heroes once had someone lose their cool at them in the most dramatic way when, in a crisis of confidence, he threw his laptop at the head of the Power Player. Most people would have gone nuts, but not this Power Player. He just handed over his own laptop and said, 'Wanna throw this too? Chuck it if it makes you feel better, because I need you at your best. If a couple of broken computers will get us there then that's fine by me.' The laptop-thrower calmed right down, apologised and, with a tear in his eye, said, 'I can't seem to locate my talent. I'm frustrated and petrified at the thought of letting you down.' The Power Player said he had every faith in him and that if he just took a breath and calmed down, his talent would come flooding back. Of course it did, and the work he produced was nothing short of spectacular. The Power Player knew that by disarming the guy and getting him to admit to his frustration, he would open up, face his fear and then get on with it. It was a beautiful move to watch.

DO YOUR JOB

POWER PLAY FOR WORK

The truly powerful and influential don't try to duck their job. They don't outsource, delegate, share or do any of the fancy buzzwords that HR people use to describe what is essentially the crafty avoidance of one's job. Many a powerful person has faked it to the top, but true Power Players don't need to fake anything. They don't leave a to-do list for someone else, but take immense pride in knowing how to deliver on their job description. It's like those old-school CEOs of media companies who started off as journalists, and if push came to shove could still file a story in a war-torn capital in order to make a print deadline. These Power Players know that an enormous amount of kudos comes from seeing the Big Boss doing the exact job of a junior. A honcho must also understand every division of the company: doing your job means sometimes knowing everybody else's job as well.

▶ THE STORY

This is the greatest story I'll ever witness: the managing director of a prestige car brand was visiting a showroom for his weekly catch up with his managers and salespeople. In walks a customer who desperately needs a flat tyre changed. With the service team all busy with booked-in jobs, this customer walks up to reception and starts practically begging for help: she needs to get to an important meeting. The front desk aren't being especially helpful and the customer is getting more stressed by the minute. Sitting in his beautifully furnished corner office in a four-thousand-dollar suit, the managing director sees that something is up and walks over to reception to ask the customer what she needs. He walks with her to the car, removes his fancy jacket, rolls up his sleeves, pops open the boot and starts changing the tyre. Best call to action I've ever seen.

KNOW WHO'S REALLY RUNNING THE PLACE

POWER PLAY FOR WORK

Power Players know that the real power in every company lies with the people who keep it running behind the scenes, and the first thing they do is seek these people out. Why? Because they are gold. I'm talking about the personal assistants who ruthlessly control access to their bosses, the receptionists who work the front desk of any business, and the dispatch team and office managers who really make stuff happen. True influencers understand that these people (supposedly low on the totem pole) hold the key to power, yet they are often treated badly by the so-called 'important' people—a big mistake. Just try teaching yourself how to use the binding machine when you're under pressure from a big deadline. Find out who does the real work and cozy up.

▶ THE STORY

The last CEO I worked for used to bypass the fancy white-tablecloth lunches with bigwigs and instead take the dispatch guys (average age: nineteen) to the local all-you-can-eat place, and this was a company with three thousand employees and a pretty significant hierarchical distance between the CEO and the dispatch kids. These quarterly lunches reaffirmed the idea that the best way of finding out exactly what's happening in a company is to talk to the people in the trenches. It's a great story that should happen more often.

⬆ MAKE SURE YOUR WORD IS SOLID

POWER PLAY FOR EVERYWHERE

If it comes out of your mouth in the form of a promise or a commitment, you need to deliver on it. This one is not negotiable: you said it, you do it. So much in the world today is moveable and malleable. So much is contingent on five other people agreeing. The real influencers know that if they've given their word, it's stronger than oak. No blaming some freak reason for why it can't happen or be delivered. Even if Power Players need to move heaven and earth to follow through, they will and they do. It's one heck of a motivational tool, too. It's not just the big stuff we're talking about here either. The stuff you might think is no big deal *is* a big deal—saying you'll do it and then not delivering is the very thing that makes it so.

▶ THE STORY

My best story on this one? I worked with a guy who was ordered by his CEO to arrange meetings with some of the most powerful media executives in New York for our biggest client. The guy (on the fast track to becoming a Power Player) said, 'Absolutely, consider it done'—and he did! He managed to get meetings with the heads of each of the broadcast networks as well as a bunch of other impressive names. He made his word oak and didn't stop until he delivered.

LOOK GOOD EVERY SINGLE DAY

POWER PLAY FOR EVERY DAY

Now this one seems pretty obvious but I'm going to spell it out anyway. Power Players always put time and energy into looking good. I once worked with a terrific Power Player who always wore the coolest limited edition sneakers with his hipster suits. It worked for him—and everyone knew to look down at his feet and see what type of footwear he had on. I've also met CEOs who look like they shop at the charity store. Too many would-be Power Players think that when they get to a certain point in their careers they can opt out of the whole looking-good thing. They can't, and neither can you. Even when you're having a lazy day and you're tempted to turn up at the office looking 'lived in', stop yourself. Not only will you inspire others to step up, but you'll also perform better.

► THE STORY

I was having one of those 'I have no talent' days. Self-loathing and hatred was starting to kick in and I had a full day of meetings ahead. The lazy road would have been to wear the comfortable jeans and sweater—clothing comfort food when ice-cream isn't within reach. Instead, out came the big frock and the big hair and the big heels: I dressed the part and the day wasn't so bad after all. I know that on that particular occasion, clothing turned my whole day around. First comes clothing, then comes attitude, then comes the good day you never thought you'd have.

DO ALL YOU CAN TO PUT PEOPLE AT EASE

POWER PLAY FOR WORK AND PLAY

Those who wield power and influence do everything they can to make people feel relaxed. They don't enjoy making others squirm; nor do they get a rise out of watching people sweat. They learned long ago that when people feel safe enough to let down their guard it helps them produce the very best they have to give. The trick to putting people at ease is pre-empting what they might need (glass of water) and how they might feel (nervous, flustered, unsure). Find people you admire who do exactly this and learn from them. It's a little bit of sunshine watching someone put somebody else at ease not for any ulterior motive but simply because it's a cool thing to do.

► THE STORY

I once sat in on an interview with a Power Player who was looking to fill a more junior position on her team. This young man who was interviewing for the job was absolutely terrified. He tripped over the chair, dropped his papers and was nearly apoplectic by the time the interview had begun. The Power Player decided to tell him a story about going to a fancy restaurant with her boss and walking out of the bathroom with her skirt tucked into her underpants. When she got back from the ladies' room to the table, her boss leaned in tactfully to tell her. It was a funny story and a kind gesture and the young man being interviewed relaxed immediately; his mishaps seemed like little league stuff compared to the skirt-in-undies incident.

AROUSE IN OTHERS THE DESIRE TO BE GREAT

POWER PLAY FOR WORK

Having real influence means being able to inspire those around you to greatness. My Power heroes always make me want to reach for the stars and I am constantly trying to find ways to show them that I'm on the case. I care deeply about what they think and how they view my ideas. In return, they seem to bring out my creativity and drive, which makes me like them more. There is an unspoken magic the truly powerful possess that can make you become your best self. How do they do it? It's simply by believing that the people around them do in fact have the very talents that are required to deliver something special. There's no greater power than when someone believes you can do it. Now that's real magic.

► THE STORY

I once had a terrific young guy working for me who wanted to be great, and the best way for me to arouse this greatness was to stop with the teaching and start with the doing. There wasn't anything I could say that could make him step up to greatness so it was time to throw an elbow. On the morning of a breakfast meeting with a CEO I decided to 'oversleep' and let my guy take it on his own. It was a big meeting intended to get a big project across the line with a big fee attached; nothing short of greatness was going to be enough. Between his desire to be great and the importance of this meeting, he was indeed great. 'Fantastic,' said the client, 'a big idea that we absolutely love and he did a great job.'

⬆ NEVER TAKE SOMEONE'S DIGNITY AWAY FROM THEM

POWER PLAY FOR LIFE

Power Players don't play the shame game—it's tacky and it's cruel. If somebody has said something wrong or made a mistake, and if they're a halfway decent person, then they already feel bad enough. There's rarely the need to rub salt into the proverbial. Power Players let people keep their dignity. Transgressors will always thank you for it and will usually remember it for a long time to come. When it's been a tough day, dignity is usually all that's left, so don't be the final nail in someone's coffin. If they've screwed up and screwed up huge, lend them a lifeline. Be a friend, or at the very least be kind and decent.

▶ THE STORY

I was in a meeting with a young guy I'd just hired, several very high-powered clients, and our CEO. The newbie was asked his opinion on a logo design and he gave it earnestly and openly, in the process deeply offending practically everyone in the room and generally making a colossal mess of it. After the meeting was done, the CEO didn't get mad, which he could have. He simply asked me (as the transgressor's boss) to have a quiet word to him about taking the measure of a room before weighing in so boldly. The newbie fell in love with the CEO then and there and it was never mentioned again. It was a class act by the CEO, who could have used the event to score cheap points or make the newbie's life hell, but he never did and he never would. This is what made him a true Power Player.

FEEL THE VIBE IN THE ROOM

POWER PLAY FOR WORK

Yeah, I know this one sounds a bit wheatgrass shot and museli, but real influencers can almost immediately take the temperature of the room once they've walked into it. It's 8.30 am Monday and in an all-staff meeting you're called on to say something about the week ahead. If the room feels sluggish and non-responsive, now is not the time to get all Anthony Robbins on them; trying to Awaken the Giant Within will simply be met with scorn and cynicism (the giant must be roused carefully on Mondays). Better to tell the truth—something like 'let's get on with it'. No need to get out the pompoms, just an honest acknowledgement of a lack of energy and motivation can turn around a room. People often appreciate a soft sell, and powerful types know this and can gently nudge people in the right direction.

► THE STORY

I had to attend a business dinner where there was a bit of a set script between my business partner and I; however, the minute we sat down to the table the vibe was off. If we'd gone with the 'script' the dinner would have been a calamity, but instead we let the conversation take its own course and quickly worked out that our dining companion was in an awful mood because he'd had a terrible day; what we were going to ask for would have pushed him over the edge. Reading the temperature within the first few minutes and being able to improvise is key to staying alive in business.

EVERYONE LOVES HEARING HIS OR HER OWN NAME

POWER PLAY FOR LIFE

I know it's simple and it's cheesy but nothing sounds sweeter to the human ear that having someone speak your name. If you're bad at remembering names, get good at it. Come up with whatever mnemonic device you need. Power Players acknowledge each person individually by name and don't try to get around it by collectively addressing people (unless, of course, there's fifty people in a room).

▶ THE STORY

One of the most impressive things I've seen was when an old and incredibly powerful major honcho turned up to a meeting with perhaps ten people present, all of whom were in awe of him and thrilled to be there. He shook everyone's hand and introduced himself (as though they didn't know who he was!) and of course they introduced themselves too. Throughout the course of the thirty-minute powwow, he addressed each person in the gathering by name. Watching their young faces light up with unbridled pride, joy and excitement made it to my top-ten list of really cool things I've seen in my business life, all because a Player remembered everyone's names. I tell you, he could have robbed a bank or sold his kids and these guys would have still tried to find a way to think well of him.

⬆ LET OTHERS DO THE LION'S SHARE OF THE TALKING

POWER PLAY FOR WORK AND PLAY

The genuinely influential don't seem to speak much at all. They are economical with their words and choose them carefully. They enjoy giving over the stage and find ways to gently encourage others to speak up instead. Power Players understand that most people like to tell their stories and have the floor, but they rarely get the chance to. Allowing somebody else to speak while saying very little yourself is not only a gracious act but also shows that you're not interested in hogging the limelight and are secure in your own persona. Many people find this hard to do. Real Power Players find it easy. That's how you know the difference.

▶ THE STORY

I have absolutely no story here except to say this: letting others talk takes a load of pressure off you!

⬆ USE THESE FOUR POWERFUL WORDS: 'DO ME A FAVOUR?'

POWER PLAY FOR WORK

Power Players know that when they need something done, 'do me a favour?' works like magic. I've seen it used when someone forgets to do their job or fails to follow through. Rather than berate them, Power Players ask (again) for it to be done by saying something along the lines of, 'I know you're busy, but if you get a moment can you please do me a favour?' It's a very nice way of saying, 'Goddamn it, you've forgotten and I'm giving you a chance to get it done properly this time.' Being asked to do someone a favour makes the recipient of the request seem special, like the boss has singled them out for this very important mission. It's funny how four little words can turn around somebody's whole world when they're struggling—and that's exactly why Power Players use them.

▶ THE STORY

I worked with a guy who thought he was untalented and useless. He wasn't; he was just going through a rough patch. Our boss would give him little jobs to do and always asked for these jobs to be done by way of a favour. They were always tasks that he knew the guy could do and do well. Little by little he helped build the guy's confidence back up and soon he was as good as new. Four magical words . . .

➊ DON'T TRY TO MOULD SOMEONE IN YOUR IMAGE

POWER PLAY FOR WORK AND PLAY

Now this one separates the posers from the real McCoys. Truth is, most of us want to create a disciple in our own image. We love the idea of building a person from scratch; I'm guilty of it, many of us are. But Power Players don't take it personally when the people they help along the way choose not to take their advice or follow in their footsteps. I've seen many a pretender sideline a junior for choosing to go his or her own way. If you've trained somebody or taken the time to steer them gently, the only thing they owe you is the truth. If they would prefer to take another road, then good for them for having the guts to do what will make them happy. The right and only response from a Power Player is to buy them a bottle of great champagne and wish them luck on their journey. If they've learned anything from you, one day the junior will pay it forward with somebody on their team. And don't be surprised if you cross paths again sometime and the baby (now all grown up) tries to find ways to repay the favour.

► THE STORY

I once tried to mould (manipulate, really) a man who worked for me because we had a similar style to begin with. Not only was I pretty arrogant in wanting to do this but I also would have suffocated this man's own style and strengths. The trick here is not to pass off this type of manipulation as 'training'. It's wrong and that's all there is.

WHEN IT'S ALL FALLING APART, TAKE BACK COMPLETE CONTROL

POWER PLAY FOR WORK AND PLAY

The most talented Power Players I've ever met all know when to step back in and take complete control. They only do this when the whole thing has gone off the rails, and never step in too early or too late. They also stop themselves from saying 'here's where you went wrong' or 'here's what you should have done'. They fix the problem and, in doing so, they teach by example. Everyone in the team (by this stage terrified and more than a little bit humiliated) will watch your every move very closely and see what they should have done instead.

▶ THE STORY

A lawyer friend of mine, who is one of the most graceful Power Players I've come across, put his very talented, experienced and highly paid team to work on a company float without him. At the eleventh hour as they were about to lodge the prospectus, the client picked up a major mistake, and this one key error led to a litany of others. Unsurprisingly, the client was livid: no prospectus, no float, no refund for the filing fee to the local stock exchange. Game over. When alerted to the problem, my lawyer friend simply put down the phone. He took a breath. He walked into his team's 'war room' and said, 'We've got a big problem with the prospectus. We work around the clock until it is perfect. We divide ourselves into two teams doing the exact same work so that we can crosscheck everything we do.' No angry words, no hissy fit, no finger-pointing, just a guy who took back complete control when it was absolutely necessary.

⬆ FAKE HIGH ENERGY WHEN YOU NEED TO

POWER PLAY FOR EVERY DAY

This one I love. There are days when the last thing you want to do is be the one to provide the energy. It's incredibly hard to do and often worthy of an Academy Award, but real influencers know that one of the most effective Power Plays is to create energy where there is none to be had. I've seen some powerful types who would have preferred to have root canal than walk into a certain room, but the moment they entered they transformed the place with a much-needed dose of energy. Sometimes the best antidote to bad ideas and a bad attitude is the performance art of high energy and enthusiasm, and this is why Power Players often get the great jobs. Take that acting course that you've been thinking about doing. It's not nuts—it's the cost of doing business (and living) in the twenty-first century.

► THE STORY

I watched an exhausted, worried and flattened friend and colleague walk into the office, place her bag on her desk, take a deep breath, and then walk straight into a workshop with fifteen people and put on the best show I have ever seen. Though I know for sure this was the last place she wanted to be, she was magnificent. She was funny, she was energetic and she put on the performance of her life. When faking it is the best you can do then go for broke. Make it worth the effort required and treat it like show business.

SAVE A DROWNING PERSON

POWER PLAY FOR WHENEVER YOU CAN

Power Players always save people from making arses of themselves, be it in a meeting, at a dinner, at a Christmas party after drinking too much, or after accidently trying to pick up the boss's wife. Why? Because we're all human and we all do things we shouldn't do or say things we shouldn't say. Who hasn't kissed a colleague (or worse) at a Christmas party, or behaved badly in the photocopy room? Power Players can usually see the train wreck coming and get their colleague out of harm's way before it becomes urban legend, knowing there is nothing to be gained from letting the situation ride. Even if the person is a complete dick and deserves whatever lawsuit is coming his or her way, humiliation as a form of retaliation is a crappy way to go. Power Players know that their role in life is to help others when they can.

► THE STORY

My boss pulled the greatest save I've ever seen when a junior got so hammered at a work function that he was seconds away from throwing up. My boss saw, put his arms around the guy (in a matey, jocular way, making it look like they were headed off to have one of those deep and meaningful chats) and led him to the bathroom where he could complete a gold-medal hurl. It was a top and thoroughly humane save. Everyone has at some point drunk too much and wished to God there was someone there to save them from deep shame and the need to move to Alaska.

TRUE POWER DOESN'T RELY ON POWERPOINT

POWER PLAY FOR WORK

I read somewhere that 'PowerPoint is the last refuge of the weak and feeble'. If it were up to me, PowerPoint would be illegal, like speeding: you get a fine in the mail and you have to pay it or you get demoted. Harsh? Sure. But real Power Players know what they are talking about, and they don't need an antiquated and predictable display to convey it. Power Players make certain that their presentations count. They shoot for just twenty minutes of talk-time and allow themselves a little visual theatre to bring their narrative to life. Short, sharp, illuminating information doesn't need more than twenty minutes and Power Players are given extra points for pith. True Power Players are fantastic storytellers. The liberation that comes from losing PowerPoint is a big step on the road to becoming a real Player. Try it as soon as possible.

▶ THE STORY

A presentation I once saw blew my mind. The presenter got up and spoke for twenty minutes without so much as a single PowerPoint slide. All he had was a beautiful speaking voice and a black marker to make some key points on butcher's paper. He was enthralling and had the entire room eating out of the palm of his hand. I loved being in the room that day and as long as I live I shall never forget it.

BE AGELESS

▸ POWER PLAY FOR EVERY DAY

Power Players, even when biologically ancient, often come across as ageless. They keep up with trends and pop-culture buzz because they know that to live well in the business world they need to know what's happening in the actual world. It's never beneath a Power Player to know about the Kardashians or Snooki or *Shameless*. Though on the surface this stuff might seem like worthless information, it's an outstanding barometer on the cultural tastes of any society. By making the effort to keep up with products, services and information that every generation is into, these Players become ageless. Just because Power Players get rich doesn't mean they have to get snobby. There is nothing more intoxicating than a serious Power Player who knows why Lana Del Rey is such a polarising superstar. And then if they want to go to their favourite restaurant and drink up a bottle of 1946 Château Pétrus, bully for them.

▸ THE STORY

My sixty-four-year-old yoga teacher has more edge that most of the twenty-two-year-olds I know. She reads everything, watches everything and tries everything. Yes, she looks amazing (yoga has a way of doing that) but her agelessness has much more to do with attitude and energy. Plugged in and connected, she is a part of the Zeitgeist and loves pop culture as much as any thirteen-year-old. Take a leaf out of the sixty-four-year-old's book: growing old doesn't mean growing ignorant.

RESIST THE BANDWAGON

POWER PLAY FOR WORK AND FAMILY

There comes a moment in every boardroom or debate when the bandwagon of popular opinion finds its momentum. Often that popular opinion is convenient but it's not always right. True Power Players resist the temptation to leap onto the first bandwagon for the sake of expediency. They have a fantastic way of seeing through the maze of directions and opinions and getting to the truth. This goes as much for people as it does for strategies. If someone is flavour of the month, Power Players don't do the same and ignore other perhaps less popular types. They are even-handed and thoughtful, both with their intellect and with their patronage. Bandwagons come and go. Searing insight that leads to the right decisions is forever. And resisting the tendency to play favourite with colleagues is priceless.

▶ THE STORY

I made a monumental screw-up, the type that gets you media coverage for all the wrong reasons. Clients ran from me, friends were no longer, enemies threw it around for sport, but one guy got on a plane and flew to my city, showing up at my doorstep and saying, 'I'm not going anywhere. This too shall pass.' He did the hardest thing you can do: he resisted the bandwagon and swam against the tide, backing me up when everybody else bailed. It's difficult to keep your own counsel when everything and everyone around you is telling you to cut and run. But he didn't. He stuck around. And I shall never forget it.

DON'T FIGHT THE FIGHT WHEN YOU'VE ALREADY LOST

POWER PLAY FOR WORK AND PLAY

It's truly painful to watch someone fighting for an idea or a direction in a meeting when the fight is already lost. This is a mistake that a Power Player never makes. Not only is it a waste of precious time and political capital, but it also looks pretty dumb. Power Players are realists and they know that losing gracefully is not only an art form but also part of the responsibility that comes with power and influence. There's no shame in losing but there's a lifetime of shame in being a sore loser. One of the classiest CEOs I know gave one of the best losing speeches I've ever heard. He said, 'We just lost out on a huge project, and we didn't lose by a little bit. We lost huge. We're losers, fair and square, no excuses. No philosophical crap either. Let's remember what this feels like so that we are never here again.'

▶ THE STORY

This is a story about love, because the same principles apply. My friend met a girl and fell in love. The girl did something very bad and they broke up. My friend convinced himself that it was fixable, but the relationship was doomed from the very moment she did it. The whole relationship was over the first time he broke up with her but he wasted years on something that was never going to be salvaged. Don't do what he did. Don't fight the fight when you've already lost.

↑ WATCH THE BODY LANGUAGE

POWER PLAY FOR EVERY MINUTE OF EVERY DAY

Power Players know that body language can give them away quicker than anything else. They control their quirks and mannerisms so that no one knows what they're thinking until they say it out loud. Slouch and you look like you've already lost. Place your arms akimbo and everyone thinks you're angry. Gaze downwards and it looks like you're having a crisis of confidence. Look up and you're either uncertain or just plain lying. Body language speaks volumes. It can also inspire confidence and show a sense of great calm. Even when things are going very wrong, true Power Players never use their body language to exploit, boss, hurt or humiliate. Watch your body language in the mirror. Get to understand just how much information your body language can communicate and make certain your body doesn't betray you.

▶ THE STORY

I am, on occasion, a compulsive hair twirler. Always have been, ever since I was a little girl. Anyone who knows me well also knows I do it only when I am completely unhinged and thoroughly unglued. Every single one of us has a 'tell' and hair twirling is mine. So now I keep the hair twirling to a minimum because my entire body language changes when I do it and it scares the crap out of everybody. Better for me to use words to tell them what's wrong with me (which I am grown up enough to do) than twirl and say nothing.

WITH GREAT POWER COMES GREAT RESPONSIBILITY

POWER PLAY TO TATTOO ON YOUR FOREHEAD

People say this all the time because it's true, and Power Players are always aware of the responsibility that comes with power. When they enter a room it can feel like Moses parting the Red Sea, and they know their words carry extra kilojoules. This is why they are careful with their words. For aspiring Power Players, remember this very important piece of advice: once you start to have some power in a room your words and actions pack twice the punch, so don't use this power badly. It may not be fair that you need to be twice as careful as everyone else in what you say, but that's the price you pay for power. Practise this: when someone does something boneheaded, choose not to be that final nail in his or her coffin. Either find a way to help them or shut up. That's real power.

▶ THE STORY

We all know people who have crossed us. I have one person in mind right now who did something so craven and unforgivable that I used to go to sleep at night dreaming up revenge fantasies. My favourite one involved backing two huge trucks up to his beach house and emptying the contents of the house into them so that when he arrived home not a single thing would be left. When I met his mother many years later, I said nothing. I had the power to forever change his relationship with his mother, get him fired from his job and basically ruin his life. But doing any of those things would make me a far worse person than he. Great power absolutely comes with great responsibility, and it often means we have to temper our reactions so we don't become the very thing we loathe.

KNOW WHEN YOU'VE WON AND NEVER BRING IT UP AGAIN

POWER PLAY FOR LIVING WELL

Power Players never gloat. Winning is only sweet when you don't make others feel bad about losing. Power Players also have this square in their heads: every time you win, you just increase your odds of losing the next time around. Power Players know it's not their job to praise and celebrate their own success. It's their job to take that success and use the momentum it has created for the next job or project. I've often listened to the power-seeking wannabes who relive every second of their win because they fear it will be the only win they ever have. Power Players let it go (and yes, they probably remember it fondly on tough days) and then gear up for the next big thing they need to do.

▶ THE STORY

My favourite boss of all time won perhaps the biggest advertising account in the country, pretty much single-handedly. He devised the strategy, wrote the pitch document, created the in-room presentation, even came up with the creative idea, and then at the eleventh hour, chucked it all out, started again and (unbelievably) came up with something even better. About a dozen people claimed victory for the win and talked about how much they'd contributed to the work. The boss said absolutely nothing, never corrected anybody, never mentioned the role he had played and never brought up that win again. Not one word. Pretty cool right?

GET SOME CHARISMA

POWER PLAY FOR WORK AND PLAY

Luckily for most Power Players, the charisma thing comes naturally. Explaining charisma is a bit like that old phrase about pornography: 'I can't define it, but I know it when I see it.' Power Players know when to use the charisma card because they were born with quite a bit of it. They understand that when there are no answers and no clear path, a little charisma can go a long way. I think the trick to this one is being comfortable in your own skin and having a sixth sense for when to turn on the charm and when to do absolutely nothing. I don't know if you can learn the charisma thing but I do think you can learn to fall in love with yourself a little bit and then the charisma things comes naturally. We all have a reserve of charm somewhere—the trick is locating it and knowing the best times to let that flair rip. When you're in the presence of a charismatic Power Player you feel a little bit loved. Crazy? Sure. But it feels a lot better to be around someone like that than not. And the thing about life (and business) is that we all want to be around people who make us shiny and happy.

▶ THE STORY

One of my favourite charisma moments was watching a chief executive cross the street on a rainy day and share his umbrella with a would-be client who was about to get drenched. The gesture oozed charisma and the way he gently took her briefcase in his hand to keep it from getting soaked almost made it a Hollywood moment. Thoroughly charismatic and I know that she thought so too—and still does, to this day.

BACKBONE

POWER PLAY FOR WORK

There are so many ways in today's business world to avoid making the tough decisions. You can hire people to do an 'efficiency study' in order to downsize, you can render absolutely no opinion on a situation and let people wallow in a pool of indecision, or you can take a 'personal day' and avoid the whole damn thing. The easiest way you can spot a Power Player is by the amount of backbone they exhibit. They make the tough calls, they don't disappear when important decisions need to get made and, better still, they shoulder the responsibility for whatever goes down. Basically, they regularly show an excellent dose of spine. Backbone is a quality all too rare in the corporate jungle. Take a lesson out of the Power Playbook and look to grow some backbone of your own.

▶ THE STORY

My dad was a fan of the backbone. He once stood up in church and questioned the priest's rather unsupportive position on a war halfway around the world in what was then Yugoslavia. Every single person in that church was thinking the same thing as my dad and murmurs of overwhelming support echoed his words. At the time I was a little kid but I still remember thinking how brave he was. Though some might argue my dad should have waited until after the mass, I'd argue that backbone is only backbone if it happens in the moment when it is most required. On this day the congregation burst into applause, and the following week the priest apologised to the congregation for not realising that the very thing keeping these people going was a belief that their faith would see them through the war. Backbone can be hard to find, but when you've shown some you wonder why you don't do it more often.

LOSE THE NEED TO BE NEEDY

POWER PLAY FOR LIFE

The powerful and influential never look needy or seek lots of attention and praise. This is an especially attractive quality and a powerful statement about self-containment. In other words, Power Players can take care of their own feelings and their own needs without relying on a team of fans or, worse, a sycophantic entourage stroking their ego or fulfilling their every wish. Don't misunderstand: this doesn't mean that they are emotionally perfect or have some type of comic-book strength. It means they have a healthy sense of self and can pick themselves up off the floor when it all goes to hell. That's an incredibly useful quality to have and it's much envied, if you ask me. Classy, too.

► THE STORY

I think it's bad karma to share someone's needy story so I'm not going to do it. All I want to say is this: don't confuse needy with asking for help when you need it.

JUST KEEP MOVING

POWER PLAY TO STICK ON YOUR WALL

My dad used to say it a lot (with a heavy Croatian accent), but Power Players know that sometimes it's all you've got. That goes double in a crappy week where everything unravels at warp speed, your heart gets broken into a million tiny pieces and life feels unhinged. In any career, there will be times when it all feels impossible, and Power Players are very aware of how quickly things can unspool. What sets them apart is that when things go to hell they have the capacity and mental fortitude to just keep moving, even when they feel like curling up in the foetal position with their thumb in their mouth. This power tip goes on the wall: *just keep moving*. Even if you have to act your butt off, even if you can't stand the thought of doing what needs to be done. Don't overthink it. Just keep moving.

▶ THE STORY

I broke up with my boyfriend in the morning. I dropped a pair of diamond earrings down a street drain at lunchtime. I ran over a cat, whose owner was close by with his two small children and who started yelling, 'Murderer!' I crashed my car (my fault: I ran into a brand new Maserati) in the afternoon on the way to an incredibly important meeting. I arrived at the meeting miraculously on time and all I wanted to do was literally fall into a heap on the floor and bawl my eyes out. But what lay ahead was a command performance to the board. At that very moment my dearly departed dad's words in his thick accent came into my head: 'Just keep moving.' I walked into that room and owned it as I acted my butt off and did my job.

⬆ DRAW THE BEST PEOPLE TO YOUR INNER CIRCLE

POWER PLAY FOR WORK AND PLAY AND IN EVERY SINGLE WAY

This is a tip that Power Players have perfected. They know that they need to have people far, far better than them in order to run the show. Recruit the very best, even if it stretches the budget, stretches the friendship, stretches your ego. The most effective Power Players I know learn very quickly what their shortcomings and foibles are and then recruit the shortfall. The most talented Power Players I know make an easy peace with the idea that their 'subordinates' are actually more talented than they are. It shows true grit to employ smarter and better. My employees always were and when I look at where they are now, I feel a little bit vindicated that I was a decent judge of talent. To rise to the rank of Power Player, remember this: it is petty and cowardly to employ less than what you are. It speaks volumes about your character, and the concrete sets very quickly when it comes to reputation.

▶ THE STORY

I can tell you with almost complete certainty that the really, really successful people (many of them world famous) got that way because they surrounded themselves with people far more talented than they are. The last four CEOs I worked under all had an executive team who kicked their arses intellectually; they knew it and they sought it. They only felt comfortable with their team when they knew they were the dumbest person in the room. In any of the businesses I've thrown some money into, I've always funded people far more talented than me. If you're ever going to have any power in the room, people must be able to trust your opinion is coming from a place of honesty rather than some ploy intended to pump up your personal 'brand'.

LOSE THE HABIT OF BEING A CLASSIC AVOIDER

POWER PLAY WE ALL NEED TO LEARN

I'd lay money that roughly twenty percent of marriages happened because one person in the couple avoided the break-up conversation and got married instead. The very best of the best Power Players break their classic avoider habit early. In fact, the absolute best ones put all their crappiest problems at the top of their to-do list. Power Players know that even if they avoid the toughest stuff, it still sits squarely in the mind sucking up precious mental real estate. This is a Power Player exercise worth adopting: every day, put the toughest job at the very top of your to-do list. If you can fast-track through the (often imagined) fear, loathing and pain of a gig you think is hard, it becomes much easier to do.

▸ THE STORY

My favourite story on this Power Play is about a CEO I know who, first thing Monday morning, asks his top people to tell him the nightmare problems the business is facing. He picks the worst and tackles it that same morning. Brave? Crazy? Humiliating? All of the above, but also a fantastic Power Player move.

NEVER ARGUE WITH A DRUNK OR A FOOL

POWER PLAY FOR EVERY DAY

This is old-school advice that you'll hear from anyone over the age of sixty. Okay, seventy. It's also excellent advice that Power Players learn early on in their careers. Professional disagreements (also known as arguments) can only happen with people who are sane and sober. Power Players know never to get into an argument with an unreasonable, scrambled or drunk mind. There are people who simply can't handle a disagreement, and Power Players can smell these people as soon as they enter a room. Even if the fool (or drunk) baits them, they sidestep the argument because it will inevitably descend into an abyss of crazy. Power Players can size up the other guy pretty quickly and don't even try to engage. Never ever argue with a drunk or a fool. This tip will save you at least once a month.

▶ THE STORY

The most elegant sidestep I've ever seen came from a close friend. Her boyfriend at the time had had way too much to drink and he started to be loud and more than a little out of control. Most girls would have stormed off huffily or made some type of scene, but my friend knew better. She let his drunken behaviour run its course, was gentle, loving and didn't get into it with him in the middle of the restaurant. My friend was the sober one and, because of this, it was up to her to think calmly for both of them. No matter what, never argue with a drunk or a fool.

FORTUNE DOES INDEED FAVOUR THE BRAVE

POWER PLAY FOR WORK

There's an old Croatian saying my parents passed on that roughly translates as 'shut your eyes tightly and jump'. Power Players know that all the research, workshops and resilience training in the world can never replace a courageous decision. It turns out that brave is in short supply in corporate Australia. I'm not talking kamikaze here but simply about the courage it takes to make a firm, concrete decision and see it through. Obfuscating is not a character trait that Power Players possess. They know that at some point they need to close their eyes tightly and jump into the unknown. The most accomplished Power Players have given up on absolute answers and certainty—there's no such thing in life. They learn to trust their instincts to make the last ten percent of that jump to the other side. Try it the next time you need to make a brave decision.

▶ THE STORY

I'm in a meeting with a guy who runs a promotions company. He's pitching to become the primary supplier of promotional gear for a major Australian sporting league. The head guy from the sporting organisation has an idea for a particular product he'd like to feature on their website that my guy knows nothing about. It's clear that the deal is on the line. My guy says, 'Absolutely, we can get that product for you. We'll work it out, whatever you need.' Of course, he had no idea where to source the product or, if he could source the product, if he could get it in time. I loved the way he dived in without a safety net because he had absolute faith that he could work it out. Diving in makes it fun and is one of the things that stretches you.

CONFIDENCE IS GOLD

POWER PLAY FOR WORK AND PLAY

Power Players radiate a type of confidence that is incredibly attractive. Not the sort that is arrogant, the kind that makes you feel that everything is under control. Aspiring Power Players work on their confidence game because they know that confidence is a critical ingredient when leading a team; people in that team need to believe that their power-playing leader knows what he or she is doing, because we all like to follow people who know where they are going. Many of us worry that if we flex our confidence muscle we'll come across as smug or cocky, but being a confident, articulate, decisive Power Player isn't smug—it's exactly what is required to become a well-regarded leader. Start exercising your confidence skills today and get used to sounding authoritative and speaking up when it comes time to lead. No great Power Player ever got to the top by being shy or coy, and indecision is a highly unattractive quality in any would-be leader.

▸ THE STORY

The confidence thing at work is obvious, but the confidence thing in a relationship or family is harder. My best girlfriend has three kids under the age of five and she just goes about her day with a great sense of calm and fun. Her confidence is a beautiful thing to watch and I honestly believe that her kids feed off this vibe. If you don't know what you're doing, how can anyone else have faith? For my friend it all comes down to knowing that she is a great mum. She is amazing at it and this self-belief is enough to fuel her through the really tough days.

IMPOSSIBLE? NEVER

POWER PLAY FOR LIFE

It's a big word. What's more, it's usually an opinion and rarely a fact. When Power Players hear the word impossible, they're already ten steps ahead, trying to figure out ways to make it possible. If you ever want to separate a room into two groups, lob the word 'impossible' into a conversation and see what happens. Power Players' heads start working on how to make the impossible go away. They think aloud, ask why, and then put together a blueprint in their heads on how to solve the problem. On a larger scale, what this says about Power Players is that they are perpetually set on positive. Their eternal optimism gives them the edge in pretty much every business situation because their default position is one of possibility and promise. Impossible really means nothing to Power Players and that's a valuable lesson for all those aspiring to become one.

▸ THE STORY

A friend of mine wanted to become a trader, so he did. Given that to become a trader you have to take a bunch of tests, work without a salary for a long time and then lose a bunch of money as you learn how to do the damn thing, it really is an impossible dream for most people. Not him. It never occurred to him that he couldn't do it, he just found a way to. And he's still doing it. Impossible? Never.

LOOK FOR THE COUNTER-TREND

POWER PLAY FOR WORK

Power Players keep their power by looking in places where others don't think to look. While the herd chases down an idea in one direction, the greatest Power Players look in exactly the opposite direction. In business we all know there are trends and fat opportunities, but the biggest paydays tend to come from the unexpected and the surprising. Power Players develop an internal originality compass and, like a good Hollywood car chase, they take a left when everybody else goes straight ahead. If you're looking to perfect your Power Player groove, get used to seeking out the counter-trend: see the opposite, the unseen and the opportunities that turn leaders into legends. Practise on a problem staring you in the face right now and get a handle on your internal originality compass. You'll be amazed at the ideas that come into your head.

► THE STORY

A global dairy client wanted me to develop a new low-fat yoghurt brand for the market. Why? Because all the market research studies told him that 'low-fat' and 'health' was 'on trend'. What I went in recommending was the exact opposite: the most full-fat, rich, decadent, buttermilk ice-cream product we could possibly develop. We priced a litre of it at twenty dollars and only sold it in oil-rich Middle East countries. The company made more in one month with this product than the entire year's projected revenue for the low-fat yoghurt. Look for the counter-trend and knock yourself out.

DO SOME DEEP BACKGROUND ON YOUR AUDIENCE

POWER PLAY FOR WORK

Sounds a little CIA, but the really impressive Power Players always have a decent chunk of background on a person they're meeting for the first time because they know that it's smart to know who's sitting across the table. Relax: this isn't about being nosy and stalking someone, it's about caring enough to understand who this person is. It's also extremely flattering when someone takes the time to find out a little bit about you, like meeting somebody new at a party who is more interested in talking about you than themselves.

► THE STORY

I recently went to a meeting with a Power Player who I think is pretty scary. His assistant took me to wait in his big fancy office and when he walked in he said, 'Full-fat latte with half a sugar, right?' To this day I still don't know how he found out. He then went on to recite parts of a speech I once gave at a breakfast many years ago and made me feel like I was the only person in the world. And that's exactly what background information does: it makes the Power Player charm and, in the process, disarm. Know your audience just a little bit better than everybody else. It's the best preparation you'll ever do.

KNOW WHEN TO TAKE SOME TIME OFF

POWER PLAY FOR WORK AND PLAY

Power Players don't get sanctimonious about the occasional day off. Taking the day off can be magnificent for the soul. When you're working at a million miles an hour and need to be at the top of your game, stopping for a day of sleeping in, catching a movie or just watching TV all day can be incredibly restorative. The world won't fall apart if you step off the merry-go-round for a day. It can be the best way of getting back some much needed perspective or having some good old-fashioned fun without a deadline. And it's often in those moments of doing nothing when the best ideas come and you find your centre. Power Players have always known this and it's saved them (and their careers) more than once. Try it. Get good at it. Not only is it fun but it will reset your head too.

▶ THE STORY

The best self-imposed time out I ever witnessed was by one of my best friends. He'd been working eighteen-hour days for three months straight, weekends too, compounded by bad food, no exercise and no life outside of work. He was completely burnt out. Finally he took a week off (not an official holiday: he told his boss that if he didn't like it he could 'retire' him) and did absolutely nothing . . . and everything. He slept in. He went for a run. He watched marathon television. He rang his friends and family. He had absolutely no schedule and simply went with the flow, and he loved it. He also realised that although he loved his job as a corporate lawyer, he would either negotiate more help or he'd leave. When he went back to work his boss was so relieved he gave him the help he needed, fearful that such great talent would walk out the door.

⬆ PICK THE MOST TALENTED (AND OFTEN LEAST EXPERIENCED) PERSON

POWER PLAY FOR WORK

Power Players know that recruiting well is a tough needle to thread. Getting it wrong means your instincts are off, and then there's the problem of what to do with a bad recruit when they fall short. The great Power Players recruit talent over experience almost every time. Power Players know if the talent base is there, teaching new recruits is relatively easy. Power Players also know there's ambition in going for raw talent over the nice experienced types and that what every business needs is the bright-eyed, bushy-tailed kid who dreams big dreams. Take a leaf out of the Power Player Playbook and identify the talented ones early. The rest you can teach. And by the way, teaching's the job of a great Power Player too.

▶ THE STORY

No story. Pure opinion.

➊ POWER PLAYERS ALWAYS WRITE IT DOWN

POWER PLAY FOR WORK

Power Players know to always get it down on paper. If it isn't written down, forget about it. There's that great scene in *Jerry Maguire* where Jerry's fiancée (played by Kelly Preston) says to him, 'It's not trust my handshake, it's make the sale! Get it signed.' And that's some of the best advice any Power Player can receive. When it really matters, get it down on paper. From a contract to an instruction manual for the new kids, don't assume people get it. When Power Players make big plays they make sure it's written down somewhere, creating a record of events if nothing else. It's like those people who talk about having a great screenplay inside them: Power Players don't talk about the screenplay, they get it down and then go sell it. If it matters, always write it down.

► THE STORY

There's a billion stories I could tell you, but the worst I've heard is about a guy who with his business partner created one of the most successful snack food brands in the country. The business partner registered the trademarks, told him they were equal partners and they worked like dogs for six months. When it came time to formalise their arrangement the business partner kept saying they'd get to it, and not to worry. You've probably already worked out the way this story went: the business partner had created a company of which he was the sole shareholder and then flipped the company to a venture capital group for a bundle of dough. The guy tried to sue his business partner. It took a year of his life and a lot of dollars, and in the end he took a small settlement out of court because he couldn't afford to keep on fighting. Get it down on paper. Get it signed.

SAY NO, RESPECTFULLY

POWER PLAY FOR WORK (BUT MORE USEFUL AT PLAY)

Power Players don't see anything magnanimous about being a martyr to the cause. They don't feel the gravitational pull of being a people-pleaser. If it isn't right, or even if it just doesn't *feel* right, they don't do it. Learning how to say no with great elegance and panache is a skill that Power Players learn early on in their careers. They can say no and it still sounds positive and charming. They don't get roped into doing the stuff that will push them over the edge. They don't go down the guilty road and turn to self-loathing when they can't fulfil every request thrown at them. Saying no is a very powerful tool in the Power Player Playbook. Do it gently and directly and never with any malice or anger. If you want to be a Power Player, go to the nearest mirror and practise saying no, kindly, gently, directly and honestly. Feels good, doesn't it?

▶ THE STORY

Do you really need one? Just say no.

FORTUNE DOES INDEED FAVOUR THE BRAVE

POWER PLAY FOR WORK

There's an old Croatian saying my parents passed on that roughly translates as 'shut your eyes tightly and jump'. Power Players know that all the research, workshops and resilience training in the world can never replace a courageous decision. It turns out that brave is in short supply in corporate Australia. I'm not talking kamikaze here but simply about the courage it takes to make a firm, concrete decision and see it through. Obfuscating is not a character trait that Power Players possess. They know that at some point they need to close their eyes tightly and jump into the unknown. The most accomplished Power Players have given up on absolute answers and certainty—there's no such thing in life. They learn to trust their instincts to make the last ten percent of that jump to the other side. Try it the next time you need to make a brave decision.

▶ THE STORY

I'm in a meeting with a guy who runs a promotions company. He's pitching to become the primary supplier of promotional gear for a major Australian sporting league. The head guy from the sporting organisation has an idea for a particular product he'd like to feature on their website that my guy knows nothing about. It's clear that the deal is on the line. My guy says, 'Absolutely, we can get that product for you. We'll work it out, whatever you need.' Of course, he had no idea where to source the product or, if he could source the product, if he could get it in time. I loved the way he dived in without a safety net because he had absolute faith that he could work it out. Diving in makes it fun and is one of the things that stretches you.

CONFIDENCE IS GOLD

POWER PLAY FOR WORK AND PLAY

Power Players radiate a type of confidence that is incredibly attractive. Not the sort that is arrogant, the kind that makes you feel that everything is under control. Aspiring Power Players work on their confidence game because they know that confidence is a critical ingredient when leading a team; people in that team need to believe that their power-playing leader knows what he or she is doing, because we all like to follow people who know where they are going. Many of us worry that if we flex our confidence muscle we'll come across as smug or cocky, but being a confident, articulate, decisive Power Player isn't smug—it's exactly what is required to become a well-regarded leader. Start exercising your confidence skills today and get used to sounding authoritative and speaking up when it comes time to lead. No great Power Player ever got to the top by being shy or coy, and indecision is a highly unattractive quality in any would-be leader.

► THE STORY

The confidence thing at work is obvious, but the confidence thing in a relationship or family is harder. My best girlfriend has three kids under the age of five and she just goes about her day with a great sense of calm and fun. Her confidence is a beautiful thing to watch and I honestly believe that her kids feed off this vibe. If you don't know what you're doing, how can anyone else have faith? For my friend it all comes down to knowing that she is a great mum. She is amazing at it and this self-belief is enough to fuel her through the really tough days.

IMPOSSIBLE? NEVER

POWER PLAY FOR LIFE

It's a big word. What's more, it's usually an opinion and rarely a fact. When Power Players hear the word impossible, they're already ten steps ahead, trying to figure out ways to make it possible. If you ever want to separate a room into two groups, lob the word 'impossible' into a conversation and see what happens. Power Players' heads start working on how to make the impossible go away. They think aloud, ask why, and then put together a blueprint in their heads on how to solve the problem. On a larger scale, what this says about Power Players is that they are perpetually set on positive. Their eternal optimism gives them the edge in pretty much every business situation because their default position is one of possibility and promise. Impossible really means nothing to Power Players and that's a valuable lesson for all those aspiring to become one.

▶ THE STORY

A friend of mine wanted to become a trader, so he did. Given that to become a trader you have to take a bunch of tests, work without a salary for a long time and then lose a bunch of money as you learn how to do the damn thing, it really is an impossible dream for most people. Not him. It never occurred to him that he couldn't do it, he just found a way to. And he's still doing it. Impossible? Never.

NEVER ARGUE WITH A DRUNK OR A FOOL

POWER PLAY FOR EVERY DAY

This is old-school advice that you'll hear from anyone over the age of sixty. Okay, seventy. It's also excellent advice that Power Players learn early on in their careers. Professional disagreements (also known as arguments) can only happen with people who are sane and sober. Power Players know never to get into an argument with an unreasonable, scrambled or drunk mind. There are people who simply can't handle a disagreement, and Power Players can smell these people as soon as they enter a room. Even if the fool (or drunk) baits them, they sidestep the argument because it will inevitably descend into an abyss of crazy. Power Players can size up the other guy pretty quickly and don't even try to engage. Never ever argue with a drunk or a fool. This tip will save you at least once a month.

▶ THE STORY

The most elegant sidestep I've ever seen came from a close friend. Her boyfriend at the time had had way too much to drink and he started to be loud and more than a little out of control. Most girls would have stormed off huffily or made some type of scene, but my friend knew better. She let his drunken behaviour run its course, was gentle, loving and didn't get into it with him in the middle of the restaurant. My friend was the sober one and, because of this, it was up to her to think calmly for both of them. No matter what, never argue with a drunk or a fool.

⬆ LOOK FOR THE COUNTER-TREND

POWER PLAY FOR WORK

Power Players keep their power by looking in places where others don't think to look. While the herd chases down an idea in one direction, the greatest Power Players look in exactly the opposite direction. In business we all know there are trends and fat opportunities, but the biggest paydays tend to come from the unexpected and the surprising. Power Players develop an internal originality compass and, like a good Hollywood car chase, they take a left when everybody else goes straight ahead. If you're looking to perfect your Power Player groove, get used to seeking out the counter-trend: see the opposite, the unseen and the opportunities that turn leaders into legends. Practise on a problem staring you in the face right now and get a handle on your internal originality compass. You'll be amazed at the ideas that come into your head.

▶ THE STORY

A global dairy client wanted me to develop a new low-fat yoghurt brand for the market. Why? Because all the market research studies told him that 'low-fat' and 'health' was 'on trend'. What I went in recommending was the exact opposite: the most full-fat, rich, decadent, buttermilk ice-cream product we could possibly develop. We priced a litre of it at twenty dollars and only sold it in oil-rich Middle East countries. The company made more in one month with this product than the entire year's projected revenue for the low-fat yoghurt. Look for the counter-trend and knock yourself out.

⬆ DO SOME DEEP BACKGROUND ON YOUR AUDIENCE

POWER PLAY FOR WORK

Sounds a little CIA, but the really impressive Power Players always have a decent chunk of background on a person they're meeting for the first time because they know that it's smart to know who's sitting across the table. Relax: this isn't about being nosy and stalking someone, it's about caring enough to understand who this person is. It's also extremely flattering when someone takes the time to find out a little bit about you, like meeting somebody new at a party who is more interested in talking about you than themselves.

► THE STORY

I recently went to a meeting with a Power Player who I think is pretty scary. His assistant took me to wait in his big fancy office and when he walked in he said, 'Full-fat latte with half a sugar, right?' To this day I still don't know how he found out. He then went on to recite parts of a speech I once gave at a breakfast many years ago and made me feel like I was the only person in the world. And that's exactly what background information does: it makes the Power Player charm and, in the process, disarm. Know your audience just a little bit better than everybody else. It's the best preparation you'll ever do.

KNOW WHEN TO TAKE SOME TIME OFF

POWER PLAY FOR WORK AND PLAY

Power Players don't get sanctimonious about the occasional day off. Taking the day off can be magnificent for the soul. When you're working at a million miles an hour and need to be at the top of your game, stopping for a day of sleeping in, catching a movie or just watching TV all day can be incredibly restorative. The world won't fall apart if you step off the merry-go-round for a day. It can be the best way of getting back some much needed perspective or having some good old-fashioned fun without a deadline. And it's often in those moments of doing nothing when the best ideas come and you find your centre. Power Players have always known this and it's saved them (and their careers) more than once. Try it. Get good at it. Not only is it fun but it will reset your head too.

▶ THE STORY

The best self-imposed time out I ever witnessed was by one of my best friends. He'd been working eighteen-hour days for three months straight, weekends too, compounded by bad food, no exercise and no life outside of work. He was completely burnt out. Finally he took a week off (not an official holiday: he told his boss that if he didn't like it he could 'retire' him) and did absolutely nothing . . . and everything. He slept in. He went for a run. He watched marathon television. He rang his friends and family. He had absolutely no schedule and simply went with the flow, and he loved it. He also realised that although he loved his job as a corporate lawyer, he would either negotiate more help or he'd leave. When he went back to work his boss was so relieved he gave him the help he needed, fearful that such great talent would walk out the door.

PICK THE MOST TALENTED (AND OFTEN LEAST EXPERIENCED) PERSON

POWER PLAY FOR WORK

Power Players know that recruiting well is a tough needle to thread. Getting it wrong means your instincts are off, and then there's the problem of what to do with a bad recruit when they fall short. The great Power Players recruit talent over experience almost every time. Power Players know if the talent base is there, teaching new recruits is relatively easy. Power Players also know there's ambition in going for raw talent over the nice experienced types and that what every business needs is the bright-eyed, bushy-tailed kid who dreams big dreams. Take a leaf out of the Power Player Playbook and identify the talented ones early. The rest you can teach. And by the way, teaching's the job of a great Power Player too.

▶ THE STORY

No story. Pure opinion.

POWER PLAYERS ALWAYS WRITE IT DOWN

POWER PLAY FOR WORK

Power Players know to always get it down on paper. If it isn't written down, forget about it. There's that great scene in *Jerry Maguire* where Jerry's fiancée (played by Kelly Preston) says to him, 'It's not trust my handshake, it's make the sale! Get it signed.' And that's some of the best advice any Power Player can receive. When it really matters, get it down on paper. From a contract to an instruction manual for the new kids, don't assume people get it. When Power Players make big plays they make sure it's written down somewhere, creating a record of events if nothing else. It's like those people who talk about having a great screenplay inside them: Power Players don't talk about the screenplay, they get it down and then go sell it. If it matters, always write it down.

▶ THE STORY

There's a billion stories I could tell you, but the worst I've heard is about a guy who with his business partner created one of the most successful snack food brands in the country. The business partner registered the trademarks, told him they were equal partners and they worked like dogs for six months. When it came time to formalise their arrangement the business partner kept saying they'd get to it, and not to worry. You've probably already worked out the way this story went: the business partner had created a company of which he was the sole shareholder and then flipped the company to a venture capital group for a bundle of dough. The guy tried to sue his business partner. It took a year of his life and a lot of dollars, and in the end he took a small settlement out of court because he couldn't afford to keep on fighting. Get it down on paper. Get it signed.

SAY NO, RESPECTFULLY

POWER PLAY FOR WORK (BUT MORE USEFUL AT PLAY)

Power Players don't see anything magnanimous about being a martyr to the cause. They don't feel the gravitational pull of being a people-pleaser. If it isn't right, or even if it just doesn't *feel* right, they don't do it. Learning how to say no with great elegance and panache is a skill that Power Players learn early on in their careers. They can say no and it still sounds positive and charming. They don't get roped into doing the stuff that will push them over the edge. They don't go down the guilty road and turn to self-loathing when they can't fulfil every request thrown at them. Saying no is a very powerful tool in the Power Player Playbook. Do it gently and directly and never with any malice or anger. If you want to be a Power Player, go to the nearest mirror and practise saying no, kindly, gently, directly and honestly. Feels good, doesn't it?

▶ THE STORY

Do you really need one? Just say no.

↑ PLAY THE TAPE THROUGH TO THE END

POWER PLAY FOR WORK AND PLAY

Power Players always think about how the plays they make are going to end. Even though they know that it may not always go exactly to plan, they still have a pretty decent idea of what might happen, scoping out the scenarios and mentally preparing for whatever might come their way. This is a trademark Power Player move. Knowing how the roads might diverge and where each ends is incredibly useful in making the right decision. Every action has a reaction and every decision has a consequence, and Power Players always remember that. Play the tape through to the end and have a loose plan in your head for what to do next. You'll be amazed how powerful this will make you.

▶ THE STORY

You snap at a competitive co-worker who doesn't like you. He retaliates and you decide to return the vitriol. You know he's itching to make you look bad and this fuels your rage. Rewind. If you'd played the tape through to the end you'd have realised that there's no way this ends well and you'd be much better off killing your competitive colleague with kindness. If you do snap and he retaliates, apologise. Wind it back and make peace. This works just as well with prickly family members.

⬆ MAKE GANGSTA MOVES WHEN YOU'RE STUCK IN THE MUD

POWER PLAY FOR WORK

Power Players get gangsta when the momentum has all but stalled. And when I say gangsta, I mean exactly that: almost illegal (but still within bounds), guns blazing, a little bit subversive and, if necessary, covered in a good dose of crazy. When the project is stuck in the mud, Power Players get tough, get decisive and get moving. The gangsta move is a licence in straight talk and action, and the power of it is that it is unexpected in business today. What it's not is a free pass in appalling manners and aggression. When Power Players use gangsta, they exhibit all the big moves without the attitude. The next time you find yourself stuck in the mud with no idea how to get unstuck, try some gangsta. If it helps, watch *The Untouchables* again, especially the parts with Sean Connery. Trust me.

▶ THE STORY

It was an all-day workshop going nowhere. The whole room was deflated; energy was low and apathy was beginning to set in. By midmorning the workshop facilitator had pulled the plug and ordered five taxis, and we all piled in. The whole workshop was about helping a bookstore chain survive in the digital-everything economy, so we went to one of the stores and were given big drawing pads and markers. We walked around and came up with ideas, talking to customers and being generally out there. The gangsta move really got our creative juices flowing.

RE-INVENT YOURSELF BEFORE THE MARKET DOES

POWER PLAY FOR LIFE

Power Players have an incredible sixth sense for knowing when it's time to do a Madonna. They are experts in personal reinvention because they know that keeping an edge helps to keep their power buzz going. Power Players know what most of us suspect: that we should evolve ourselves before others find us predictable, repetitive and, worse, dull. Even when Power Players reach a lofty place, they never lose sight of the fact that they also need to evolve. They know that if the market determines they are past their use-by date, they are toast, and it's their job to make sure they never get there. If it is time to change your modus operandi, do it before you are obsolete. Reinvent brand You if you have to. Power Players do this all the time.

▶ THE STORY

This story isn't about work at all. But it is about reinvention. A woman I admire dedicated the first part of her life to work and more work. The world saw her as all work and no play, no private life. The concrete had set. And then all of a sudden she reinvented herself, unleashing her knockout body on the world and starting to date up a storm. She fell in love, got married and then decided to change careers altogether. Total reinvention, and totally terrific.

CALL AN AUDIBLE

POWER PLAY FOR WORK

For those readers who don't watch US pro football, 'calling an audible' is a football term that means changing the play based on what you see the other team doing, and it's one of the hardest things to do in a game. Power Players are masters at calling an audible. In business this is the equivalent of spontaneously changing the strategy with the potential client sitting on the opposite side of the table. If the brief or the game changes right before your very eyes, you have to learn to hustle and come up with some brilliance on the spot. This is a sure-fire way to fast-track your trajectory to Power Player status.

▶ THE STORY

The best audible I ever saw was by a CEO who realised five minutes in that his rehearsed pitch was totally and completely wrong. He gathered up the documents, threw them in the bin and asked the client what they really wanted from the company. He turned the meeting into a live Q&A and it was thrilling to watch. It was totally in the moment: crazy, fantastic, high energy. Power Players are genius at calling an audible.

GIVE GREAT EMAIL

POWER PLAY FOR ANYONE WHO EVER SENT AN EMAIL

Power Players are the greatest emailers this side of the information superhighway. Whether it's pith that's required or a cracking one-liner, Power Players send the most fantastic emails. You know you're in the presence of greatness if someone has a Power Player's email printed out and stuck on the wall. The usual sign is that they write their emails in headlines, smart, wry, funny and warm. If email scares you or if you shy away from the medium, start practising now. Get comfortable in the medium. Send a few to yourself; give them the overnight test and see how they read in the morning. So much great stuff can be communicated in an email and so few of us are talented at them. Understand what you communicate in tone and personality when you send one. Here's one more thing: ditch the *War and Peace* emails and get lean with the language. It will elevate you from a 'potential' to a 'sure thing' Power Player.

▶ THE STORY

Best email I ever got from a Power Player? An email containing one word: 'Freak.' I emailed an important document at 3 am that I had written in one night, and that was the response I received. Perfect, warm, and a little bit admiring. Power Players keep the emails short and funny.

➊ PHILANTHROPY IS PART OF YOUR JOB

POWER PLAY FOR WORK (AND LET'S TRY IT AT PLAY)

Natural Power Players see generosity and philanthropy as part of the job. What's the value in having power unless you can do some good with it? Power Players always have enough heart to build some philanthropy into the mix. Although it feels good in itself, giving isn't about being a do-gooder. It's about reminding all the people who work with or for you that there will always be people whose lives are much, much harder. Power Players know that when they stop seeing the world through other people's eyes and see only their own lives, they lose their gratitude and they forget about the bigger picture. Make time for philanthropy, but don't make a big deal out of it. That's the Power Player Secret Handshake Code of Conduct.

► THE STORY

Giving isn't giving if it comes with a megaphone and a press kit. An old friend makes sure that the local soup kitchen knows to come to him if they are short a thousand bucks here or there. I only found this out when the local priest was in the same café as this friend and me and wouldn't let us pay for our coffees; when a priest pays for your coffee, you ask questions. So I asked the priest how he knew my friend and he said, 'Max is our credit card—that we don't have to pay back.'

➊ BUY THE PLANE TICKET FOR A FIFTEEN-MINUTE MEETING

POWER PLAY FOR WORK

Power Players are outstanding at taking the minimum amount of time to make the maximum impact. Power Players know something you don't: if you believe in it enough, no decision is too crazy.

► THE STORY

A Power Player I work with flew from Sydney to Perth and back in one day for a fifteen-minute meeting. Everyone in her organisation thought she was nuts and yes, to the ordinary observer the meeting would have looked like a long shot, but the potential client was incredibly impressed with the effort, commitment and respect demonstrated. That two and a half thousand bucks on airfare, the money on taxis and the time invested were the best this Power Player ever spent. It became the crossroads piece of business for her company and proved to her entire team than fifteen minutes is all that's needed when you believe in what you are doing.

ACT LIKE A SMALL BIZ EVEN IN A BIG BIZ

POWER PLAY FOR WORK

Power Players know that size isn't everything. It's like those oversized genetically engineered strawberries: huge, but no flavour. Take a leaf out of the Playbook from Power Players at the big end of town. They might preside over a large business but they still roll like they work in a small business. Terrible things can happen when little businesses become big: they can lose their gumption, their soul and their humour. The world's greatest Power Players (at that Warren Buffett level) might be giants, but they still play the game in a small business way, like thanking someone personally, walking the corridors to chat to the people in cubicles rather than the corner offices, having lunch at the cheap place rather than the sixty-dollar main course restaurant. Big might be beautiful in Texas or the porn industry but it's generic in the world of business.

► THE STORY

Every week, the CEO of one of Australia's biggest mining companies still goes out to the mine, puts on a hard hat and does a couple of hours with a bobcat. He started at the very bottom working the mine, and he never wants to forget what it feels like to do an honest day's labour. The reaction from the guys on the ground is extraordinary. They tell him what's really going on, improvements he should consider, safe shortcuts they might consider making. He is in one of Australia's biggest businesses and he still acts like it's a small business, like the boss in any small business does when he or she licks the stamps in the morning and does the big-cheese stuff in the afternoon.

ANTICIPATE, INTERPRET, DECIDE

POWER PLAY FOR WORK

Great Power Players have that freaky gift of knowing how to anticipate. Before something becomes a big, fat problem. But it doesn't stop there. They also know how to interpret, to read between the lines. Once they've got all the information, they make concrete, accurate decisions. Anticipate, interpret, decide: three of the hardest words in business and ones most people can spend a lifetime and a career avoiding. Good anticipation means you're well prepared for whatever comes your way and puts you ahead of the competition. Power Players know if you misinterpret, you're in a whole world of pain, but get it right and you're reading someone's mind. Making a decision becomes much easier when all the information is in and accurate. Watch how the Power Players you know anticipate, interpret and decide.

► THE STORY

My boss knew that our client was coming to fire us. Everybody else said he was overreacting. My boss knew differently—that we would be the first to go in a tough economy. While everybody else avoided any thought of a contingency plan, my boss already had one in his pocket. Sure enough, the client told us the entire marketing spend had to be cut; the product wasn't selling so well. My boss said that was the last thing they should do, and that marketing and advertising was exactly what they needed to withstand the economic downturn. My boss said, 'Give us fifteen percent equity and we'll do the work for free for the next two years; after that we'll renegotiate.' Talk about anticipating and deciding. The client went for it and that fifteen percent earned our company more money than all their other business combined.

GIVE FEEDBACK ON THE SPOT

POWER PLAY FOR WORK

Power Players are terrific at incorporating feedback the moment it's required. Don't stockpile or wait for that so-called appropriate moment that may never come. Power Players know that helping good talent become great is the way to keep the best minds, and it's also the right thing to do. If you intend on becoming a real Power Player, seize every opportunity to give constructive advice to those who seek your guidance and counsel. The trick here, of course, is to do it with kindness and tact. Giving feedback gently is a talent that the best Power Players hone early on in their careers, and they know that the best lessons happen in the moment. On the spot feedback is gold, and means Power Players grow a loyal team who seek their help and incorporate their lessons into their daily work. On the spot is where it happens.

▸ THE STORY

I worked with a smart young woman who was a terrible presenter. She'd use five hundred words when fifty would do and had this awful habit of burying the lead. I'd give her feedback on the spot in private rehearsals by showing her how else she could tell the story, and after a while she became a fantastic presenter.

GIVE EVERY EMPLOYEE A CHANCE TO BLOSSOM

POWER PLAY FOR WORK

Some of the greatest talent started off pretty wobbly, and many of the finest Power Players can remember one person who gave them a chance to really blossom when the rest of the jury was out. Power Players give every single one of their employees a chance to truly blossom. A Power Player I admire greatly once gave me the best advice on this: 'Most people, when given the space to show their talent, step up and rarely disappoint.' Give everyone a shot at being better—everyone. The greatest Power Players will tell you that when they gave their unlikeliest candidates the chance to blossom, they were very happy with the results.

▶ THE STORY

When I started in my first strategy job I had absolutely no idea what I was doing. I felt that too much had happened too soon (mail room to TV production to strategist, all in four months). Thankfully, I had a wonderful boss who taught me how to do everything but also let me have those days where I was totally freaked without making me feel like I was a loser. She threw me into the deep end of the pool but she was always only an arm's distance away from pulling me out if I got myself into trouble. She knew that the best way for me to learn would be to give me a chance at the real work, no coffee making or photocopying. She let me grow into a person with real skills and real talents. It's a terrific way to allow someone to blossom.

KNOW THE DIFFERENCE BETWEEN ISOLATION AND SOLITUDE

POWER PLAY FOR WORK AND PLAY

Power Players get that being alone doesn't mean being lonely. Solitude is a critical ingredient in the cake called success. Power Players always make time for working and just being on their own. It's this time away from the crowd that is crucial in honing one's thinking and problem-solving skills. There's absolutely nothing isolating about sitting alone for a few hours a week—or even one hour a day—and speaking (or collaborating) with absolutely no one. On the contrary, Power Players know that people who cannot take this sort of solitude are usually high-maintenance types, and nobody thinks high maintenance is sexy. Take a cue from the best Power Players out there: plan some solitude time as regularly as you can. It's this quiet space that will provide you with the answers to life's biggest questions.

► THE STORY

One of my friends makes a point of spending one weekend out of every six totally alone, getting to know himself all over again. No girlfriend. No friends. No family. He reads, sees a movie on his own, and sometimes goes to a restaurant on his own. He treats himself to downtime. On these weekends he's off the clock and he doesn't have to perform for anyone. He just gets to have some solitude and peace, and think about his life and where he is at, whether he is happy with his choices or should be making some new ones. He is reflective and contemplative and absolutely in the moment. It's pretty impressive stuff.

THE CONVERSATIONS YOU RESIST ARE THE ONES YOU MUST HAVE

POWER PLAY PARTICULARLY FOR PLAY

Power Players seem to step up when the rest of us want to run away, especially when it comes to conversations most would rather avoid. When Power Players sense a conversation coming their way that might be a little sticky or uncomfortable, they know it's not going to go away all on its own. Instead of looking for ways to avoid it, they bring it on. They know that if the conversation bothers them that much, it's usually because it's an important one to have. Power Players also know that once they have the conversation, the bottleneck they've been experiencing usually gets sorted and everything starts to flow a lot more smoothly. Stop resisting and start facing; Power Players have the ticker to do exactly that. Give it a shot.

► THE STORY

You just know this is going to be another story about relationships. A man who lived across the street from me dated a woman for two years—the second time. The first time he dated her for three years. The first few months into the second stint, he wanted out. But he never had the conversation. It took him another twenty-two months to break up with her. When he finally did, he felt so guilty because he'd already dealt with the emotional fallout in his head and was ready to move on. On the other hand, his girlfriend was shocked. She thought they were happy. She thought he was going to propose. Have the conversation.

IF IT'S NONE OF YOUR BUSINESS, IT'S NONE OF YOUR BUSINESS

POWER PLAY FOR WORK AND PLAY

Great Power Players know when to keep their noses out of somebody else's business. If it's not their place to know or to comment or to get involved, they don't. Not ever. The classiest Power Players never try to make something their business that's not. Most of us enjoy a bit of juicy gossip or want to weigh in on someone's private business, yet Power Players rarely do. They let the momentary urge pass because they take a longer view of what this involvement might mean a month or a year ahead. There's a strange kind of power that comes from *not* knowing someone's private business. It allows Power Players to leave the judgment to one side and focus on the stuff that matters, like talent and skill. When it's not your business, don't make it your business. Ever.

▶ THE STORY

The story here is what happens when you make somebody else's business your business. A guy I sat near in an early job had a terrible habit of involving himself. He made himself a player in office intrigue and gossip and soon people began to fear him. If he sidled up to them in the kitchen, they'd smile nervously and get the hell away. Don't be one of those people. Nobody likes a nosy parker.

GET COMFORTABLE WITH CONSTRUCTIVE ANGER

POWER PLAY FOR EVERY DAY

Power Players have a healthy attitude toward anger. Not the crazy, destructive kind that ends up in handcuffs, but the kind where you need to express how you feel so that resolution can ensue. Honest anger is much better than passive aggression (you know, the awful kind where you ask someone how they are and they tell you they are fine, but they are actually pretty pissed off). When Power Players are angry, they say so. They do it immediately and, most importantly, calmly. Constructive anger can achieve a great deal in an office environment, communicating your disappointment quickly and clearly. Anger is an important emotion that we all feel from time to time, but many of us shy away from admitting it. Power Players see anger as a part of the human condition, and a realistic reaction in both the workplace and life. If it leads to honest feedback that can lead to a solution, it's a positive thing. Good anger. Get comfortable with it, like the best Power Players do.

▶ THE STORY

Once my sister and I went to visit our brother at his nice shiny law offices, and I can't even remember why but she and I got into a big fight. My brother only gets angry for good reason, but that day he lost it with us. I still remember the look on his face and the tone in his voice. He got mad and told us to knock it off, and we did, embarrassed and humiliated as he set us straight. If he'd not lost it with us the whole thing would have escalated, or he would have buried his anger and it would have emerged at some other time and place. Moreover, my sister and I were able to kiss and make up a lot sooner because the fight had been stopped short. He's a pretty great brother.

SOMETIMES YOU NEED TO JUST STAND THERE AND BE WRONG

POWER PLAY FOR LIFE

Being wrong takes a great deal of self-assurance and confidence. Why? Because you can't hide behind ego and hubris. Power Players know that being human means being wrong at least half the time. Most of us pretend that we're never wrong or, worse, we try to blame someone else for our mistakes. Power Players know that being wrong is liberating. It also creates an enormous level of trust within any team, because if you admit your mistakes most people will trust that you also know when you're right. These days, so few people admit to being wrong. When someone does, it's actually refreshing. Now don't misunderstand: this power tip doesn't advocate crying or being pathetic in disclosure, just a simple statement of fact: I got it wrong. So when you know you're right, people will trust that too.

► THE STORY

I was headhunted for a CEO gig. The chairman interviewing me asked about a boneheaded comment I'd made in the press when I was young and stupid and trying to make some noise. The minute he brought it up, I was deeply ashamed. There was a long and uncomfortable silence. What could I say? Nothing except this: 'I was young and stupid and trying to make some noise. Which means I was wrong. I screwed up.' Though I didn't end up taking it, he offered me the job. He told me that it had nothing to do with my CV, it was because I didn't try to justify my stuff-up.

SOMETIMES ALL YOU NEED IS THE ILLUSION OF POWER

POWER PLAY FOR WORK AND RELATIONSHIPS

Power Players have learned the big lesson: the difference between actual power and the illusion of power. Often, the illusion is all you need because just the whiff of some power can get a clued-up Power Player across the finish line. Inference, pretence, possibility, suggestion—these are all excellent tools when creating the illusion of power. Power Players know that most of us can't help ourselves when we get the opportunity to imagine the ending of the story all on our own. If someone implies or gently suggests, we already have the ending written beautifully in our heads. And if people believe that you have the power, they will act accordingly—sometimes when actual power isn't available, the illusion of it will do just fine. Ask any Power Player who has stretched the (power) truth when the real thing simply isn't available.

▶ THE STORY

This story might be a little suspect but I don't care—all's fair in love. And when you find somebody you love (or could love), you should fight for them. Can't get the boy/girl you like to notice you? Create the illusion that you're dating somebody else. Conniving? Sure. But it creates an illusion of power. At the very least it will make the object of your affection think twice.

DITCH THE DEMOCRACY

POWER PLAY FOR WORK

Power Players are familiar with that old Winston Churchill chestnut: 'The best argument against democracy is a five-minute conversation with the average voter.' Power Players love democracy throughout the world, but they don't love it within a business. Nothing great ever came from a democratic boardroom. The most successful companies have a clarion voice, one that is crystal, visionary and usually correct. I like to call it a benevolent dictatorship. Power Players don't try to do democracy in order to make people feel good or included, because they know it rarely works and leads to lots of workshops and tortuous discussions that result in nothing much at all. Power Players will tell you this: get your democracy hit at the next federal election. In the office, you're the leader—gracious, yes, honest, of course, but above all, visionary.

▶ THE STORY

News Corporation is a global powerhouse in print, digital, movies, TV and publishing, creating content and controlling distribution. It started with Rupert Murdoch's father, Keith, buying one small Adelaide newspaper in 1929. Whatever you think of Rupert Murdoch, he is the clarion voice in a complex company. He sets the compass. He calls the plays. Democracy isn't always the best solution.

REAL POWER IS LEAVING A LITTLE ON THE TABLE

POWER PLAY FOR WORK, BUT USE IT AT PLAY TOO

Power Players never suck all of the power out of the room; real power is leaving a little something on the table. It says many things. First, that you're not greedy. It also says you're not needy. And finally, it says that your ego isn't the size of Texas. Truly great Power Players don't need to flex their power muscle and decimate the competition. Even when the opportunity arises for Power Players to assert their power overwhelmingly, they never do it. It's ungracious and undignified, like eating everything that's put on the plate. The classy people always leave a little something on the table and eat just enough to be satiated but not full to bursting. It's a little weight- and power-management tip that only the classiest Power Players know.

▶ THE STORY

This power tip works in your personal life too. My girlfriend dated a guy for a while who always seemed to put her down. She started an online company (that he called a 'pissy little business') and did very well. He was broke and in a job he hated, but she also cleaned up his credit card debt and supported all his harebrained get-rich-quick schemes before they split up. After a while a big business bought her little business for a few million dollars. She happened upon the former boyfriend one day and learned he was still in the same job and living exactly the same life. She, on the other hand, had taken the millions, bought a home in cash and started a new business. At that moment a lesser person would have played the 'my pissy little business made me a couple of million bucks' card, but she never did that. She wished him well and went on her merry way.

ALWAYS SAY GOOD MORNING

POWER PLAY FOR LIFE

Don't you hate it when people march into the office and launch into the day without saying a single polite word? It's terribly rude, and alienating. Power Players say good morning. The work can wait for five minutes to allow for a 'Good morning—how are you?' Power Players say it at every opportunity, in the elevator to strangers or at the café ordering a double espresso. It's never inappropriate to salute someone with a cheery, heartfelt good morning. What happened to this simple courtesy, or any of the others we used to enjoy a generation ago, like letting someone merge into the traffic? Or holding the lift door open to allow a person running towards it to get on? Or helping someone carry a stack of papers, their jacket or their bag when they're teetering on the edge of dropping it all? Powers Players always say good morning. And usually, the rest of this list too.

▶ THE STORY

I was having a totally crap morning. The worst. Visions of taking a baseball bat to the nearest car flooded my mind. I grabbed a coffee from the local and the barista gave me the biggest 'good morning' ever along with a smile. Straight away I become a member of the human race again. It's these small gestures that make all the difference, and as I walked back to my house I felt my whole body relaxing. My attitude had shifted, and what ten minutes ago had seemed disastrous and unfixable now felt like no big deal. Two words and one smile was all it took for me to change my perspective and find that positive attitude.

AVOID THE PROPHETS OF DOOM

POWER PLAY FOR WORK AND PLAY

The world is full of people who drag their unhappiness around with them wherever they go. And worse, they usually tend to be very unlucky. Power Players never try to rehabilitate these people. They know these types have a terrible attitude and they will rarely change, always finding the dark cloud in a silver lining and infecting any room with their negative energy like a virus. Power Players immediately sidestep these people and you should too. It isn't your job to convince naysayers to come over to the bright side, nor it is your job to expend your energy propping up unhappy people who enjoy their pity party. It's only natural that from time to time we have a bad or sad day or lose our way, but what I'm talking about here are the toxic types who settle into their unhappy, unlucky rhythm and won't budge. Identify them early and move them on. Power Players always do and it's one of the best decisions they can ever make.

▶ THE STORY

I once worked with the unluckiest person I've ever met. Everything that could go wrong did: car accidents on the way to work, sprained ankles, bad break-ups with girlfriends, food poisoning and sunstroke. It wasn't until I spent some time with him that I realised why—he never missed an opportunity to miss an opportunity. If there was the potential for a happy ending, he'd naysay it to death. If there was the potential for some fun to be had, he'd dampen the mood. If he was presented with a chance to make a new friend, he'd point out all their faults to them. He became a magnet for the bad stuff. Learn from this guy and never go down this road.

CULTIVATE AN AIR OF CALM AND STABILITY

POWER PLAY FOR LIFE

Keeping a calm head is incredibly hard when all you want to do is scream: this is what separates the pretenders from the Power Players. Power Players do everything in the Playbook to cultivate an air of calm and stability, even when they want to hack their own arm off with a butter knife. Most of us lose our heads in moments of great stress, but Power Players know that others look to them for a reaction to guide their own. A calm, stable Power Player can influence all the others on their team to keep their heads. Here is a great tip from Power Players: every time you come up against a stressful situation, use it as a chance to practise staying calm. You'll find your work life far less stressful and your chances for success exponentially higher. It's also a very elegant reaction that will win you fans and admirers.

► THE STORY

This one's for my brother, the calmest person I've ever seen in business. As a corporate lawyer, he deals with hot-headed clients on a daily basis. It's the pointy end of business where millions of dollars can be made or lost, so some heat is understandable. This is where my brother comes in. Cooler heads need to prevail and his is the coolest I've seen. Once I sat in on a meeting with him: the clients were nuts, the bankers were even more nuts, voices were raised, accusations were flying across the room, and I watched my brother gently and carefully put the pin back in the grenade. Unbelievable. The client leaned across to me and said, 'We love your brother.' Couldn't have said it better myself.

BE THE FIRST TO KNOW, FIRST TO TRY, FIRST TO BUY

POWER PLAY FOR WORK

Power Players walk the walk. They don't stop at knowing—they progress to trying and then to buying. Power Players know that nothing beats firsthand experience. Trying, tasting, using and experiencing are critical in showing employees, customers and clients that nothing can ever replace genuine firsthand knowledge.

▶ THE STORY

I found myself at a lunch hosted by the CEO of an Aussie-owned fast-food chain. The fast-food honcho asked the round table (stacked with other rich honchos, all running marketing companies, who eat at fancy joints most nights) whether anyone had recently had one of his burgers. I watched one CEO talk in specifics about the entire product range and the fact that he'd done drive-through a few nights before. His description of the burger, fries, dessert, pricing and special offers was nothing short of enthralling. Everyone else at the table looked sheepish, not to mention snobbish, at their lack of knowledge. No surprise what happened after that. When the fast-food honcho was shopping for a new PR company, he went straight to that knowing CEO without even so much as a pitch. Be the first to know, the first to try and the first to buy.

HAVE A LITTLE FAITH

POWER PLAY FOR EVERY PART OF YOUR LIFE

Great Power Players I've known are long on faith. I'm not talking about the kind where you have to show up to church every Sunday but the kind where you keep the faith in your fellow human; faith that if given the chance to step up, most people actually do. On tough days when it's hard to get excited or feel good about, well, anything, Power Players pull out the faith card. Often the crucial step between failure and success is a little bit of faith—don't knock it 'til you've tried it. There's something very comforting about keeping the faith, even if there's absolutely no earthly reason why you should. When they're reaching for something to keep them going, Power Players look to faith. Just the act of believing that things will turn out well or that the world will right itself is enough to keep moving. Have a little faith. It will help you more than you know.

▶ THE STORY

My sister has great faith in people and, come to think of it, great faith in general. When I'm sometimes a little tough on my brother's kids, my sister comes at it from a whole different perspective. She sees all their gifts and great qualities and has a deep well of faith in their futures. And she's right: they are great kids and they are on their way, and I think that her faith in them has something to do with it. Faith: the substance of things hoped for, the evidence of things not seen. Fantastic stuff. Right up there with my sister.

DON'T BOGART THE SMARTS

POWER PLAY FOR WORK, OR ANYWHERE SMART PEOPLE LIVE

Power Players know better than to steal the smarts out of the room. Put another way? Don't claim the good thinking as your own. In any meeting there are arguably no more than two smart or original things said. Power Players are far too graceful to hog the good ideas. If you never said it, thought it up or had anything to do with its creation, don't pinch the smart. Power Players never, ever cross this line. They don't hitch their wagon to the cool kids in the room and they never elbow their way into the popular thinking. They do exactly the opposite: praise the inventor of the thinking and create more room for these smart types to run wild and weave their magic. This is a critical lesson and every great Power Player I know always plays by this rule.

▸ THE STORY

I'm helping out in a business right now where someone, let's call her Bronwyn, has come up with a terrific new model to take the business to the next stage in its development. She's smart, capable and unbelievably talented, and though she has shared the idea with me and I have the ear of the CEO and managing director, the smarts belong to her and her alone. My job in this scenario is clear: do whatever it takes to help her get the ear of the bosses and serve her in whatever way I can. Even though I'm not terrible at identifying a good idea and sharpening it up, this smart bandwagon is Bronwyn's alone.

MAKE TRIPLE-CHECK THE NEW NORMAL

POWER PLAY FOR EVERY SITUATION

If they are relying on a statistic to tell the story, Power Players only quote a stat that's been verified by three sources. Power Players know that triple-checking is the new normal in business. Not once, not twice, but three times. A lot of information gets passed around, the concrete sets quickly and it becomes fact. Often it's not. If it all hinges on the facts, make absolutely sure they are right and don't accept a near-enough statistic as good enough. Why? Power Players know there is a unique confidence that comes with knowing no one can challenge your facts. On top of that, any ideas or strategies developed off the back of that fact are solid. Solid is rare in business these days and Power Players look for any chance to deliver the solid. And the added bonus? Every time that Power Player quotes a fact, people who hear it can take it to the bank. And that's solid gold too.

▶ THE STORY

A journalist friend of mine always recites great statistics. I love it when he does. They come in the middle of an argument he is making, used as evidence for whatever theory he is putting forward. He's incredibly well read, and the evidence is always rock solid and from reputable sources, never from some fringe journal filled with bogus research. He checks his facts all the time and he never talks shit. If you're making a bold statement, for the love of Mike, base it on some facts.

DON'T LET THE URGENT CROWD OUT THE IMPORTANT

POWER PLAY FOR LIFE

Every Power Player worth their weight knows this one by heart: on any given day there will be a to-do list a mile long, but great Power Players never let the urgent crowd out the important. Power Players also know that compulsive list makers should spend time making fewer lists and more time getting stuff done, and the stuff that usually needs to get done is a short list. Two to three important things often make all the difference as opposed to fifteen 'urgent' things that won't make a lick of difference in the long run. Knowing how to tell the difference between the two is the trick and, after some practice, Power Players know how to tell the urgent from the important. Important sets the project's compass in the right direction; the urgent is simply white noise. Practising this one on a daily basis will save you anguish, time and your sanity.

▶ THE STORY

Important for me was writing this book; urgent was the long list I'd made of things to do to avoid writing this book. For five weeks after I signed my contract, I wrote not a single word. The urgent list contained everything from changing the sheets to spring-cleaning my wardrobe to sending thankyou cards for my birthday gifts to a whole bunch of work that if I'd not done would have made no difference at all. Until I went to a barbeque one Saturday night and saw an ex-boyfriend with his new girlfriend. As I watched them, I thought, Why am I here trying to be mature when the whole thing is awkward? I have a book to write. And write I did, all through the night and for twelve hours straight. Don't let the urgent crowd out the important.

A SPOONFUL OF SUGAR IS JUST SUGAR

POWER PLAY FOR WORK

Power Players know that the old adage of a spoonful of sugar making the medicine go down doesn't change the fact that the medicine still needs to be administered. Power Players understand that sugarcoating might take a little off the edge, but in the end they still need to get the dose down. They take reality (and honesty) seriously. Most of us can take truth that's told honestly and gently. What we hate is dishonesty and avoidance. Power Players might joke around from time to time and dress up the bad news when it's required, but they never run away from the tough speeches and decisions. Sugarcoating only gets you so far. Delivering medicine usually delivers respect as well.

▶ THE STORY

A very good friend got himself mixed up in some trouble and lost a lot of money to some very dodgy people. He came over one night and spilled his guts. He was hoping I'd say 'You poor thing, that's terrible.' I told him he was lucky to get out alive and to never get involved in such a sordid business again. I told him I was stunned that somebody so smart could be such a tremendous dick. He needed money: I helped him once and told him that if he ever got himself into this kind of trouble again I'd be less understanding. He cried and told me it was exactly what he needed to hear.

SUNSHINE IS THE BEST DISINFECTANT

POWER PLAY FOR LIFE

Gifted Power Players rarely hide the problems that need solving; they believe that sunshine is the best disinfectant when it comes to fixing what's broken. In other words, they open up problems and see how they can help solve them. Hiding what's broken is rarely the best course of action. Admitting there are issues also fosters a sense of trust and community. Power Players understand that there is no room for humiliation when problems need to be solved; the more heads on the case the better. There's something incredibly honourable about admitting problems out loud and proud, so throw the idea out there and see what happens. It will knock your socks off.

► THE STORY

This is about a family with a son who needed to lose some serious weight; if he didn't he would surely meet the inside of a box prematurely. For years the topic had been avoided. Gentle nudges. Hints dropped. Murmurs behind closed doors. Finally another family member opened up the topic in a full-frontal assault and said that she would take over his business for a few months if he went away to lose the weight. The topic was out in the open. The conversations were real. Emotions were running high. Terse words were exchanged. The son went away, lost an incredible amount of weight and took back the reins of his life. Sunshine really is the best disinfectant.

DON'T USE A SLEDGEHAMMER TO BREAK THE ICE

POWER PLAY FOR WORK

Power Players know to chip away gently at the relationship ice. They put the sledgehammer away because it would be like using a bazooka to kill a mosquito. Ice-breaking is a fine art and it doesn't have to happen all at once. Power Players know that it's usually awkward getting to know somebody new in business: people are guarded, unsure of whom to trust and nervous about crossing any lines. Power Players always walk softly when attempting to create a bond with someone new. Remember these three golden rules: don't get too familiar too fast, don't act like a friend when you're not, and if the person you're courting gives you a red light, stop talking before you humiliate yourself. Power Players have a deft touch with the ice-breaking skill required in business today. Watch them and learn. It's one of those terrific lessons that no business school in the world can teach you.

▸ THE STORY

It takes me years to make a real friend, through lots of small moments over time. My friendship with one friend whom I love tremendously was made in such a way; it was probably three years before we felt we could tell each other absolutely everything. We knew we were building a friendship for life and we were both of the opinion that trust is the most important thing in any relationship. Over the course of the last eight years we've built the kind of friendship that is stronger than oak. It's the type where if you were in a fix and only allowed to make one phone call, it would be to that person.

ALWAYS GIVE IT THE SLEEPOVER TEST

POWER PLAY FOR WORK, PLAY, LIFE, LOVE

Even when it sounds like it's the best idea in the world, Power Players still give the big stuff that counts the sleepover test. Power Players know that even if they absolutely positively love the idea, they should keep their mouths closed, think about something else, wake up the next morning and if they still love the idea, it's a keeper. It takes an enormous amount of self-control to keep from jumping up and down when you hear the Big Idea. But Power Players have learned this trick for two reasons: first, they get to check that their internal compass is well oiled, and second, if it's a stinky idea they can back out gracefully. Power Players know that great ideas will still be great ideas after a sleepover test and that bad ideas have a way of dying quickly after a one-night pause. Learn from the best and adopt this trick as your own.

▶ THE STORY

On a Thursday my business partner and I met a potential supplier who we thought would be fine, so we made a handshake agreement. On Friday I woke up and knew we'd made a big mistake. So did my partner. Untangling the agreement was awful and if we'd given it the sleepover test we'd have saved a lot of mess. Don't do what we did. Give it a night.

BE A SOURCE OF JOY

POWER PLAY FOR LIFE

Power Players are the people who everybody else wants to be around. You know the type: people who make you feel happy and good about yourself and make the time spent together fun. The greatest Power Players are a source of joy; people instinctively want to be their friend and love being around them. They have a naturally positive vibe and a knack of putting everyone at ease. Each of us has a choice to make in life: we can either be a source of joy or a source of misery. Power Players do everything they can to attract people to them. Even in the darkest, most awful moments they keep lightness in their step and know that a smile, a kind word and a positive disposition can make a difficult situation more than just bearable. Be a source of joy. It makes all the difference.

▸ THE STORY

My most favourite work colleague was a constant source of joy. I absolutely loved working with him and not a day goes by that I don't miss him. He brought out the best in everyone around him, including me. I always felt smarter and better and cooler when I was working with him. He could change my mood with his infectious enthusiasm and his laugh was larger than life. To this day, I don't believe I'll meet anyone who can lift me up by my bootstraps as much as he was able to. And that's pure joy.

ASK FOR THE MOON

POWER PLAY FOR WORK

When Power Players dream, they dream big. This is why they ask for the moon—just in case there's a chance they might get it. It's amazing how few of us go for broke, but Power Players are different. They don't waste time nibbling around the edges—they go straight to the top and ask for what they want. To some that might seem ambitious, and it is. But Power Players don't do it for the ambition. They do it because it's hopeful. There is something miraculous about believing that big things can happen, and it's this belief that is often the only thing standing between success and failure. Take a leaf straight out of the Power Players Playbook: next time you're in a position to, ask for the moon. You just might get it.

▶ THE STORY

When we landed our very first ongoing client in the first business I owned, we decided what the hell, we'll go for broke. They were a huge organisation and they liked the way our heads worked. We asked for a really substantial monthly retainer for research and trends forecasting. And we also asked them to pay an exclusivity fee if they didn't want us to work with their competitors. They agreed. The retainer set us up. It paid for our overheads and the contract lasted four years. Ask for the moon. Sometimes you get it.

MAKE IT LOOK EFFORTLESS

POWER PLAY FOR LIFE

The best Power Players make everything look effortless, and here's how they do it: they don't fall into the trap of heavy-handedness. Everything they do has a light touch, from the way they say hello to the way they eat their lunch. All you have to do is levitate above the situation. Rather than be in it, see yourself and the entire scene from above and that's how you make it look effortless. It's a gift and it will help you more than you can possibly imagine.

▸ THE STORY

I once watched a serious Power Player scrape the entire side of his car along a concrete pylon when parking; he'd simply misjudged the distance. His reaction? 'Well, that was entirely predictable.' My reaction? 'Oh my goodness, that's bad.' His? 'No, that's insurance.' Even when trashing his own car he maintained an air of effortlessness.

ALWAYS FORGIVE YOUR ENEMIES BECAUSE NOTHING ANNOYS THEM MORE

POWER PLAY FOR LIFE

This is one tip that Power Players love, and the best Players do it every time. Enemies thrive on discord and drama; if you take that away from them, they have to put their energy someplace else. The best explanation I heard about this was as follows: if you're having a fight with a close friend or partner and they lash out in anger and say they hate you, respond by saying, 'Well, you can hate me all you want, but I love you.' What do you think their reaction will be? You've just taken all the oxygen out of the fire and the negative flame they've given birth to cannot be fanned. Forgive your enemies—they'll be unbelievably blindsided. They won't know how to react and you'll come out smelling like a rose, and that type of power is priceless.

▶ THE STORY

There's a man I know who I'm pretty sure doesn't like me very much. Screw it—he actually hates my breathing guts. He said nasty things to get a reaction out of me and, in return, I said very nice things to him. It destroyed him that I wouldn't take the bait, and the more belligerent he was the nicer I became. Kill cruelty with kindness and forgive all your transgressors every chance you get. After a while he realised his meanness was ridiculous. I was no threat to him and all this behaviour did was make him look crazy. He'll never be a friend but he hasn't been cruel or mean since.

ABSENCE CAN BE VERY POWERFUL

POWER PLAY FOR WORK AND PLAY

Power Players know that sometimes not turning up can be more effective than being in the room. If there are people on the team who need refereeing and the Power Player they look to for resolution doesn't turn up, they are forced to sort it out themselves. Power Players are well versed in using absence wisely. Not only can it make the heart grow fonder but it also proves that other saying: less is more. Power Players don't need to be everywhere all the time. They limit their appearances to when it can make a powerful statement or to allow others to step up. On the flipside of this, when you *are* in the room, be present. There's nothing worse than a person who is physically in a room but is not really there. This is why Power Players choose absence wisely. There's always a reason and a purpose for their absence. And when they choose to be there, they really are.

▶ THE STORY

This works best at play, especially for family members that you're not crazy about but have to see from time to time. My friend has a really suspect mother-in-law who has perfected the backhanded compliment, professes to be an expert in childrearing and is full of useless advice. She is the classic know-it-all mother-in-law. My friend has in return perfected what we call the 'drive-by'. While she still has to see the mother-in-law, she does it in a way that limits exposure to her snide little comments. She'll miss the first part of the family barbeque by arriving late, or focuses on her kids once she gets there. She limits her own comments, especially when she is baited. Her absence, both physically and emotionally, works a treat. This makes her powerful and smart, and keeps her sane too!

⬆ BRING IN THE OCCASIONAL ICON

POWER PLAY FOR WORK

Nothing says power quite like a guest appearance from a great icon. Power Players keep a list of iconic figures in their Rolodex and from time to time bring one in to do the classic inspirational chat. Hearing it straight from the icon's mouth makes everything more believable: if they've lived through it, they probably know what they're talking about. That the Power Player can tap the right person on the shoulder and get them in the room is also pretty impressive. Icons remind us of what's possible, and their star wattage goes a long way in turning just another day into a memorable one. Power Players also have fun with their icon selection: the more surprising or lateral the icon, the better the value, because Power Players know that it's these unexpected moments that lift their team's spirits and transform ordinary into extraordinary.

▶ THE STORY

I was at an intimate lunch for businesswomen when into the room walks Martha Stewart. Talk about star power. Her trailblazing ways in publishing, building a personal brand and creating an empire are the stuff of legend. Her story was inspiring and the lessons invaluable as she spoke honestly about the failures and the pressures. The 'case study' of her global success was real and personal, and the mood in the room was electric. I've never seen so many seasoned women turn into groupies. Fantastic stuff.

FANTASY ROLE-PLAY CAN GET YOU THE LAST TEN PERCENT

POWER PLAY FOR LIFE

Power Players usually have a terrific imagination, so they often use fantasy role-play to get a deal across the line. Get that cheesy porn scenario out of your head: this is about Power Players projecting the fantasy victory out loud to get their people excited and motivated. Imagining the dream scenario out loud is a valuable technique in getting people to have hope that big dreams can come true. Much of fantasy role-play involves great storytelling, where the Power Player paints the picture of success. We all need to hear what victory looks like and it gives us something to hold onto when it gets tough and exhausting. Crazy, big dreams spoken out loud are incredibly powerful, and the best Power Players know that it takes this type of inspiration to get that last ten percent.

▸ THE STORY

My sister is gold at painting a picture that gets the imagination going. When I call her to report that everything I'm touching seems to be imploding, she paints a scenario where my life is a Norman Rockwell painting. It might be fantasy, but it's this story that gets me moving again. It gets me across the line in my own life and makes a believer out of me so the pathological optimism comes back and I'm back in business. Giddy up.

MASTER THE ART OF TIMING

POWER PLAY FOR EVERY SINGLE DAY

Gifted Power Players can sense good timing before they need to work with it. Not speaking too soon, not speaking too late or not speaking at all are all incredibly hard gauges to measure. Power Players know how to dance with timing so it's smooth and effortless, poetic and beautiful. They hold back when others would dive in and ruin the moment. This is perhaps one of the toughest skills to master and it takes years of looking, listening and learning. It also takes the ability to recognise when a quiet moment is needed or when to give an idea room to breathe and grow before it is critiqued. Time is a terrific fixer, healer or detonater when required. Learn how to stay out of its way and let time do its thing. Power Players always do.

▶ THE STORY

I was watching two friends get into a pretty juicy argument. None of us was quite sure what to do as it escalated into shouting. And it got worse, much worse, and then they were screaming into each other's face, noses almost touching. At any minute it could have come to blows. There was a moment of silence so tense we were all holding our breath when another friend of mine jumped in with this: 'Before you go any further, let us start a pool and put some money on it.' The timing was perfect. It diffused the situation and everybody let out one of those huge laughs, which only happen when the tension preceding is so heavy. Great timing is a gift and this fight was stopped because of it.

IF IT'S FREE, IT'S DANGEROUS

POWER PLAY FOR WORK AND PLAY

Whoever coined the phrase 'there's no such thing as a free lunch' knew what they were talking about. If something is free, odds on it's dangerous. Rarely do people give anything away for free. Even if there isn't a financial transaction involved there will usually be some other type of 'give' attached to the transaction. Random acts of kindness in business are rare, so be careful when accepting something for nothing. You might think it's free, but Power Players know there will often be a price tag attached somewhere else down the road. And if the giver of the 'free' isn't compensated in the way they would like, the receiver will forever feel in their debt. If it's free, it's dangerous. Don't accept favours. Pay for people's time when you use it, and if you need help then make sure there is a clear financial agreement in place.

► THE STORY

I once received a big basket of goodies from a client, a supposed thankyou for the work we were doing for them. It was an expensive one, full of sexy stuff: good perfume, lotions, champagne, chocolates, all manner of delicacies that cost a week's salary. A few days later the client started calling me at all hours with unreasonable requests; they'd gotten it into their heads that they had the right. That damned basket meant I had to pick up phone calls at 9 pm and go an extra ten miles when they didn't deserve so much as one. In the end, I had to fire them. That damned basket caused me headaches, and I don't even like all that fancy crap.

⬆ IGNORING TROUBLEMAKERS IS THE SMART PLAY

POWER PLAY FOR WORK AND PLAY

Power Players know that you can't please all of the people all of the time. There will always be naysayers who'd rather be passive aggressive than confront you head-on. These are the people who Power Players call the classic troublemakers, because they like the attention a fight gives them. They enjoy the spotlight, the adrenalin. The smartest Power Players do the one thing they can do when confronted with these troublemakers: they ignore them. By ignoring the troublemakers in your professional circle, you neutralise whatever power they might have. It's an effective, immediate and necessary solution, and it means that the troublemaker is forced to punch himself out when nobody is returning the jabs. This is incredibly smart and powerful, and Power Players have always known that.

▶ THE STORY

One boss of mine would question me at every turn and was masterful at throwing me off balance and implanting doubts in my head. It took me six months to work out that the best way out of it was to ignore her. She'd throw down a comment and I'd give her a thoughtful stare or a nod and then simply walk out of the room. It took me six months because I'm slow, but you don't have to be. Ignore the troublemaker and get on with your life.

IF SOMEONE HAS A PROBLEM WITH YOU, RAISE IT DIRECTLY

POWER PLAY FOR WORK AND PLAY

Just because Power Players have power doesn't mean others won't have a big problem with them from time to time. Power Players look a problem directly in the face. If someone does have issues with their approach, they don't avoid it or, worse, pretend it isn't there. They go directly to the source and they raise it with them. Power Players know that people have the right to a legitimate beef. When a Power Player goes directly to the source of that beef it demonstrates three things: humility, fairness and great character. Learn from the most accomplished Power Players and don't sweep problems under the carpet. Go directly to the person and see if you can sort it out. Nine times out of ten, it will work.

▶ THE STORY

My girlfriend is notoriously late. We agree to meet at 1 pm and she'll arrive at 2 pm. For years I'd simply built her lateness into my schedule, then one day I decided that if we were still going to be friends twenty years from now, we needed to talk about it. The next time she was late I told her that her lateness always made me feel like her time was more valuable than mine and that I didn't deserve the same courtesy of promptness that I was extending to her. It was a direct conversation had respectfully, and my friend was never late again.

DON'T LET YOURSELF GET DRAGGED INTO PETTY DISAGREEMENTS

POWER PLAY FOR WORK

Petty disagreements are part and parcel of every workplace. There's no accounting for how many times we take the low road. When petty disagreements happen, Power Players stay well away. Others will try to drag them in but Power Players have seen this behaviour before and never let themselves for two big reasons: first, it gives the pettiness legitimacy, and second, it drags the Power Player to a level that is quite frankly beneath them. The minute you take a step down you surrender the high ground and you lose your gravitas. No matter how tempting it might be to referee a petty fight or step in and take a side, Power Players never do. If it's petty it's beneath every great Power Player and the people concerned need to learn to sort it out themselves.

▶ THE STORY

I'd accidentally taken someone's parking space after starting at a new job. I apologised, moved my car and bought the guy a coffee. I thought that would be the end of it. It wasn't. The guy whose space I'd taken turned it into a mini-war. Turns out I'd been given the job he had lobbied hard for and he'd now been given a very convenient axe to grind. He sent out an email to the entire department reminding everyone to park their cars in the right parking spaces, and saying such mistakes were incredibly inconvenient and rude. Overkill, I thought, but I didn't let myself get dragged into his petty disagreement. When he started calling me 'Rosie with the fancy car', I said absolutely nothing. Everyone else thought he was a dick and the boss's decision not to give him the job was vindicated.

BLEND INTO THE CROWD WHEN YOU NEED TO

POWER PLAY FOR LIFE

Power Players need to know when to stand alone and when to blend into the crowd. Blending in is sometimes necessary to be a generous and benevolent leader, because people who work for Power Players need to cut loose from time to time. Take, for example, the notorious Christmas party: no one wants to have to worry about the boss taking notes on behaviour. A smart Power Player would do one of two things: blend into the crowd or, better still, leave the party so everyone else can let their hair down. The best ones don't wear their power openly when it isn't required and they remember how attractive an egalitarian approach can be. Knowing when to be one of the guys is a big part of being a successful Power Player.

▸ THE STORY

A great boss did the post–pitch win pub crawl with everybody else. The behaviour was outrageous: the jokes were offensive (but very funny) and crazy things were happening all over the place. The boss didn't pull seniority and was simply one of the crew, and when things got really dicey he decided it was time to call it a night. Pulling rank when there's no rank to pull makes no sense, and if you want to be a great Power Player you've got to learn to blend in.

PICK THE ROAD LESS TRAVELLED

POWER PLAY FOR WORK AND PLAY

Robert Frost knew what he was talking about: nine times out of ten, the road less travelled does indeed make all the difference. Obvious roads lead to obvious endings. Generic begets generic. Some of my favourite Power Players are great because they naturally choose the road less travelled. By taking this road they open up their world to potential magic, adventurous paths, crazy opportunities and the luck that comes with being courageous. Each of us is given a whole bunch of chances every day to take the less familiar path; Power Players get pretty comfortable with doing so. They also find it infinitely more interesting and a whole lot more rewarding. The next time you're faced with two roads, take a lead from Power Players and choose the one less travelled. Though it might be unexplored and unpredictable, it may lead you to the most interesting place ever.

► THE STORY

A guy who worked for me was terrific and talented, a little miracle in the making who could have made a million a year before the age of thirty if he'd stuck with that career path. But he didn't do that. He wanted to become a journalist, which meant starting at the very bottom as a cadet on a quarter of the salary, travelling the road less taken. He loves what he does and is becoming a beautiful writer. This road will take him to places unimagined before he quit his lucrative (safe) job and I love, love, love that he did it. He'll get his happy ending because he had the guts to go searching for it.

DON'T BE A DICK

POWER PLAY FOR LIFE

Obvious? Sure. But true. When you get the urge to jump on top of someone and act ungraciously, resist the temptation. Power Players know that it's very difficult to take things back; lash out in anger and it may haunt you for years to come. In short, don't be a dick. Nobody wants to do business, have lunch or even admit to knowing someone who behaves like a dick. Worst of all, it's a terrible slur on your reputation and something from which you never recover. No matter how much you want to throw a temper tantrum, don't. Then you're just the person who acts out and behaves like a jerk, and nobody wants to play with that guy ever again.

▸ THE STORY

Colleagues are having lunch. One reaches over to take a french fry from the other guy's plate and he gets his hand slapped and is told to 'Drop the fry'. The guy saying it is serious! It's a fry! And it's a dick move to do this. It's usually the small things that make you look small. And when you look small, you look like a dick.

↑ THINK LIKE A CLIENT TO CATCH A CLIENT

POWER PLAY FOR WORK

For most businesses, adding new business is oxygen: if you're not converting new clients, you're going backwards. Power Players know this, and this is why they spend most of their time thinking like clients. Why? Because to catch a client you need to think like one. It's amazing how few of us do this when we are pitching new business. Power Players put themselves squarely in the shoes of their client. They take an external view of their own business and how their offer appears: is it attractive? Will it do the job? Does it fall short? The only way you can catch a client is to behave exactly as they would.

▶ THE STORY

I'm working on a big pitch and I waste a week thinking like an amateur. And then it hits me. What I should be doing is seeing the whole pitch process from my client's point of view. There are going to be five agencies pitching this business, and all the strategies and creative ideas are likely to be identical. So I start to think like a client to catch a client. I'd want my agency to be original and not to kiss my arse. I wouldn't need gifts and sweet emails and attempts at catching up for some fake meeting or, worse, lunch. I'd just want them to back off and do an amazing job working out how to make my business work a whole lot better. So we did. And yep, we won.

ONLY ROLL THE DICE WHEN YOU CAN AFFORD TO LOSE

POWER PLAY FOR LIFE

Power Players never gamble unless they can afford to lose. Think of it like Vegas: never put it all on black unless you can afford to go home empty-handed. Gambling is incredibly alluring and very sexy but only if losing will not wipe you out. Power Players always, always know the odds. If you can't afford to lose, you can't afford to play.

▶ THE STORY

I've got about a million but none of them will convince you of anything until you are in the driver's seat. One day a huge opportunity will come your way and require that you take a big gamble. If you like your chances go for it, but there ain't no such thing as a sure thing. Factor in losing and—if you can still play another day—take the gamble.

HAVE A PLAN B

POWER PLAY FOR LIFE

Shrewd Power Players always have a Plan B in their back pocket, an exit strategy or trapdoor if things go south. A Plan B should never be openly discussed—the theory is that you'll never have to use it, but it needs to be in place all the same. The lesson from Power Players is this: have a contingency plan in place for that proverbial rainy day. It's smart and cool to be prepared, and the best Power Players never walk into a room without a Plan B.

▶ THE STORY

I made a recommendation to a client that unfortunately turned out to be completely wrong. My Plan B was hooking them up with a company that could solve their problem, and I refunded their money too. I also told them that if they weren't happy with the new company I'd find them another one. They were, and many years later they came back to me for another project; this time I got it right. My Plan B got me a beautiful (and lucrative) Plan A many years later.

BACK THE DARK HORSE

POWER PLAY FOR WORK

Power Players have a wonderful talent for backing the dark horse. It takes a special kind of gift to identify the long shot that will hit paydirt, and in every stack of ideas there's usually one. When it's a person, Power Players know how to identify and nurture the dark horse without the person even knowing it. Why? Because it spooks the horse. Power Players know that long shots don't need to be reminded that they're long shots, they just need to be given some confidence to hit their stride. And to keep the racing metaphor going, when they are given some space to run, they usually end up first past the post. When the dark horse has an idea, Power Players make sure the idea gets the space it needs to seed and blossom. Next time you enter a room, look around and see if you can identify the dark horse. If you're unsure, don't worry. It will take some time to learn to pick the long-shot winners in the pack. Once you get this talent down it will become invaluable.

▸ THE STORY

I'm hoping for my dark horse to break any day now. That's it, or I'll jinx it.

EAT HUMBLE PIE

POWER PLAY FOR LIFE

Power Players make peace with that awful instinct to be as arrogant as we can for as long as we can. Get comfortable with eating humble pie from time to time for three reasons: humility is a dying art and it keeps your ego in check, it's a very attractive quality and will win you respect, and it's the fastest way to put a major disaster behind you. The added benefit is that Power Players live by the adage of leading by example, and if they are willing to play the humility card, everyone else in their team is encouraged to do the same. The next time you scheme a way to blame someone else, or mount that high horse to avoid a problem altogether in the hope it will go away, stop. Slice yourself some humble pie and it will all be over. And what's more, you'll be respected for having the courage to do so.

▶ THE STORY

The downside of having power is that you can get carried away with your own sense of greatness. Once I won seven pitches in a row, and then I started to think I had a lock on number eight. I lost number eight and I lost big—it would have been bigger than numbers one through seven combined. I tried to blame it on the client, but my preparation just wasn't very good. I should have served myself up a big piece of humble pie, learned from my mistakes and incorporated it into pitch number nine. Instead I wasted two weeks avoiding the truth and sitting high on my horse. Who cares if I won seven? I lost the one that counted the most. Losing happens, but with it should come some honest self-assessment. That's where the pie comes in.

MAKE LIKE A GHOST

POWER PLAY FOR EVERY SITUATION

Power Players always know when it's time to make like a ghost and leave the room. If we really listen to our instincts, we all know when our presence isn't required. Power Players are always one step ahead and know when to remove themselves from a situation before they are asked to leave—or worse, everyone else in the room is praying to God that a piano falls on their head. Know when to be invisible. Become expert at leaving a very small footprint when you need to. Know the signs and read them. Make like a ghost when your presence is of no help whatsoever.

▶ THE STORY

Here's a classic scenario most of us have experienced. You're at a friend's house for dinner and she and her husband are about to launch into an argument. Rather than stay and provide a distraction, don't be a hero. Get out of there as soon as you can. Don't call the next day. Leave her alone until she reaches out to you, if she does at all. Never mention it. It never happened.

↑ INCREASE YOUR LUCK QUOTIENT

POWER PLAY FOR WORK, PLAY, LIFE, LOVE

Power Players know that luck is hard to come by, so they do whatever is possible to increase their lucky streak wherever and whenever they can. They think lucky, they believe they're lucky and they do whatever they can to make themselves a magnet for luck. Power Players keep lovely superstitions alive, like wearing lucky socks, crossing their fingers, wearing their watch on a particular wrist, or eating their dessert before their steak. They do all the crazy stuff they believe will keep their luck flowing. Though it might be quirky or even a little nuts, it's all about keeping the gods happy and realising that so much in life is about chance and timing and good old-fashioned luck. Take a lead from the Power Player crew. Be lucky, act lucky and do whatever you can to feel lucky.

▶ THE STORY

Before every new business pitch I do a special blessing for the group. Though raised Catholic, I'm not especially religious, but if I don't do that blessing I feel really unlucky. Evidence? Yep. The one time I didn't do that group blessing we lost. And it was one of those crowning glory pieces of business we would have loved to win. If it helps you feel successful, do it—and to heck with those non-believers who think it's ridiculous.

⬆ PULL OUT THE BIG GUNS BUT BE PREPARED TO USE THEM

POWER PLAY FOR WORK

Like boy scouts, Power Players are always prepared. If they need to pull out the big guns, they do, though they only do so if they are prepared to use them. Never pull the proverbial gun on someone unless you are willing to fire it. Every now and then, talk won't get the job done—you have to be prepared to cut loose and end whatever mess is on your desk, swiftly and decidedly. Power Players don't drag it out and they don't hope it will go away. They man (or woman) up and hit it head on, but it's never an empty gesture. If they pull out the big guns, the other person is dead in the water. If Power Players choose this course of action it is always warranted, and the decision is never taken lightly. Learn from this and do the same when you need to.

▶ THE STORY

In my first business I caught one of our assistants stealing money from the petty cash tin. It wasn't a lot, about a hundred dollars. She admitted it and apologised, and I asked her to repay the money and never do it again. This was her one get-out-of-jail-free card. I told her that if she did it again, she'd be fired. About three months later she did do it again. I didn't get angry. I didn't ask her why. I didn't offer a lecture. I just asked her to leave immediately. I didn't even let her pack her things; we sent them on the next day. If you make a threat with conditions attached, you have to follow through, and that's all there is to it.

↑ 'A LIE CAN TRAVEL HALFWAY AROUND THE WORLD WHILE THE TRUTH IS PUTTING ON ITS SHOES'

POWER PLAY FOR LIFE

Mark Twain is the reputed author of this brilliant and so-true statement. Power Players understand the brute force that a lie carries when it isn't arrested by the truth. They also know that the best way to neutralise a lie is to get the real story out there, and fast. If a lie is making the rounds, get mobilised quickly. The minute it gets repeated—or, worse, reported as fact—it's almost impossible to correct. Many a decent soul has been felled with a lie or half-truth because they thought it would go away all by itself. Getting on the front foot of a lie and telling the real story is a tactic all accomplished Power Players have in their trick bag. If the truth is at risk, don't hope for the best. Stop the lie in its tracks and use the truth to do it.

▶ THE STORY

Somebody told somebody else a white lie about me. It made its way around a staff of three thousand before I even knew it had been said. It wasn't juicy, like drugs or a saucy affair, but it was about a person who had left the company supposedly because of something I'd said. I'd never met this person, had never spoken to this person and to this day I have no idea why they left. It took about three months to unring that bell, and it only happened because people started spending enough time with me to see that it wasn't my style at all. If you get a chance to stamp out the lie early, give it a shot.

TAKE A WALK ON THE WILD SIDE

POWER PLAY FOR WORK AND PLAY

Power Players keep a wild streak in their back pocket. It's useful to pull it out every now and then because being a little nuts has its advantages. Power Players know that playing the crazy card knocks people off balance, especially when the Power Player in question has a reputation for sober, conservative, predictable behaviour. No one quite knows how to react or what to say. Shrewd Power Players also know that taking a walk on the wild side invigorates and gives them an edge when they need it most—and, truth be told, it's a lot of fun. The next time you need an ace in the hole, take a walk on the wild side. Be unexpected. Play unpredictable. You'll wonder why you haven't done it sooner and, in the process, will probably get exactly what you want.

▶ THE STORY

My work colleague and I had to attend a ball with our clients. It came with a fancy crowd and a fancy dinner and lots of appropriate behaviour. Afterwards we all decided to try a bar for a nightcap and happened upon a comedy club. Though we were a tad overdressed (we were in gowns and suits and the crowd was in thongs) my colleague and I headed inside along with our clients. It happened to be open mic night and my hysterically funny colleague, who'd had a drink or three, got up on the stage. She started riffing about 'appropriate behaviour' when with clients and without them. She had that crowd roaring with laughter, along with our clients, who saw her in a whole new way (they fell in love with her, actually). The next week at work their whole attitude had changed and everything ran more smoothly. A little walk on the wild side . . .

RECRUIT OUT-OF-THE-CLOSET NERDS

POWER PLAY FOR WORK

Power Players are closet nerds; anyone with real power usually is. So Power Players recruit other nerds. Why? Because they're smart, and usually funny (or at least dry). Nerds are also high achievers, unable to walk away from a job until it's done perfectly. Power Players are careful to recruit out-of-the-closet nerds, the ones who don't try to be cool for fear of exclusion from the hip table. They wear their *Star Trek* t-shirts openly and have a full set of *West Wing* DVDs and the lone series of *Studio 60*. When you find yourself in a position to hire talent, go for the out-of-the-closet nerds. I promise, they'll save your sanity, your reputation and they'll do everything they can to fix whatever problem comes their way. One nerd is worth five regular people—trust me.

▶ THE STORY

One of the first people I employed was a great kid called Jack. If the nerds had a king, he would have been it. It was 1999 and the internet was exploding, and we wanted to create some kind of daily email full of pop culture and trends content for our clients. He'd been told by an 'expert' that we'd need to buy a piece of software to automate the whole process that would cost us ten thousand dollars. Jack thought this was ridiculous and built us a piece of software that could do exactly the same thing for ninety-nine bucks. If not for Jack, we would have gone ahead and spent the ten thousand bucks, unaware that we were being ripped off in an era where anybody professing to know digital technology was making truckloads out of people who had no idea.

IF IT LOOKS WRONG, CALL IT

POWER PLAY FOR WORK AND PLAY

Power Players can sort out right from wrong in less than a second. Less than half a second, in fact. When it's wrong, Power Players call it immediately. They don't give it oxygen to breathe or room to run because they know that if they do, something wrong can turn into something sort of right, and sort of right is still wrong. Many a stupid idea has been backed because someone with power didn't have the guts to call it a dumb idea. Many an untalented person has been given the lead on a project because someone with power didn't have the guts to fire them. If the idea is wrong, if the person is wrong, if the fiancée is wrong, call it. Power Players do because they don't want to spend the next two years of their life trying to make it right. Watch and learn from the best. It will save you some serious pain and heartache.

▶ THE STORY

I employed two people in my team because the boss thought it would be a good idea—management wanted to show how the company took talented young people and grew them into fully fledged professionals. Problem was, these two were not particularly talented, nor were they my choice. I should have sorted it out from the beginning and told my boss that I would be happy to have more people in the team but of my choosing, but I didn't. I figured I'd work with the clay I'd been given and the whole thing was a disaster. I was deeply uncomfortable trying to train people who didn't have the X factor you need in my line of work. Both knew they were falling short but couldn't do much about it. When they were eventually fired I remember thinking, If it's wrong, don't pretend it's right.

QUASH THE POWER YOU GIVE TO REJECTION

POWER PLAY FOR WORK AND LIFE

Power Players don't ever give too much energy to rejection. They live by the philosophy that when one door closes, another door opens. Most of us lose ourselves so completely and totally when we are rejected. We spend countless hours wondering what we did wrong and focusing on every single one of our flaws. Power Players don't give rejection a voice but instead see it as an opportunity to go in another direction. Rather than dwell on all the things that haven't happened, focus on all the things that could happen. Look at new horizons rather than the roads that didn't lead anywhere. Most of all, Power Players know that rejection is something that happens to us all and the time and energy we might give to it is wasted. Better to focus on the new door that opens.

▶ THE STORY

'Balding, skinny, can dance a little' they said of Fred Astaire at his first audition. Talk about rejection. We've all got a rejection story and we all need to do what Fred Astaire did. Just keep dancing.

IF A FLAW WORRIES YOU, PUT IT OUT THERE IN PLAIN VIEW

POWER PLAY FOR WORK

Rather than hide their flaws, Power Players put them out there in plain view for all to see. They understand that the energy and time it takes to hide that flaw could be better spent on something that matters.

► THE STORY

One of the most successful Power Players I know had a habit of interrupting others when they spoke. At the beginning of every meeting he would tell people that he had a terrible case of 'speakus interruptus', and if he interrupted mid-sentence, he told everyone to tell him he was doing exactly that, and to continue speaking until they finished that thought. He also told the room that he was working on it and wanted to apologise in advance. He bravely put the flaw out there in plain view and owned up to it being an ungracious trait—and it no longer became something that everyone could judge him on. It was an interesting tactic and highly effective.

ASK FOR HELP AND ASK EARLY

POWER PLAY FOR WORK

Power Players know within ten seconds if they are out of their depth. This is approximately the same time that they ask for help. When you are out of your depth and know that you will drown, ask for help. Don't hide it, don't hope it goes away, don't wait for a 2 am miracle, just ask for help. Ask early and ask for it honestly. Don't hide the ask under a 'If you've got some time I'd love you to put your eyes over this.' Be straightforward: 'I could really use your help and would love it if we could write this document together. There are some holes in my knowledge and I need your expertise and skills.' You'll discover what most Power Players already know: people love to help when their skills are solicited respectfully and honestly. Ask for help straight up and you'll be amazed at how forthcoming this help will be.

▶ THE STORY

I had to work on a strategic plan for the pet food industry. Anyone who knows me knows that I don't know anything about cats and dogs. I don't want to know anything about them. I can't fake it. Even if I researched it, I knew I'd miss the big points. So I asked a dog and cat lover to help me out every step of the way. He considered himself a junior and didn't know why I was asking him, so I told him that on this job I would need him supervising me and not the other way around. I asked for help early before I could screw it up.

BUY STYLE

POWER PLAY FOR LIFE

There are Power Players who have a natural flair for style and there are others who suck at it. The ones who are no good at dressing well and looking good don't give up: they simply buy the style they need. They enlist a tailor, or somebody to go shopping with them to help them buy the right wardrobe for their body shape and industry, or they go to a great stylist who can recommend a new haircut. Style matters. Whoever preaches that 'it's what's on the inside that matters' is full of hooey. Style tells the world that you have good taste and a discerning eye. What you wear matters too; it always has and it always will. Even the grungy rock stars are making a point. Power Players know that if you don't feel like a million bucks (usually because you don't look like a million bucks), the day will be a lot harder to handle. Make peace with the idea that image matters and address it. Put that hard-earned money to good use and look as good as you can. Make people wish that they had that suit or outfit when you walk into a room and feel good about yourself in the process. It really does work.

▶ THE STORY

A CEO I absolutely adore always looks stunning. Every client of hers tells me that they feel better after meeting with her because it's like they've been bathed in class and style. She puts on a show simply by the way she looks, like a throwback to the fifties when wealthier women never left the house without looking gorgeous. Some might see this as sexist but to me it's a way to add beauty and style to the world. And in a world filled with a lot of ugly behaviour, what's wrong with a little extra pretty?

GET OUT OF PEOPLE'S WAY AND SHUT UP!

POWER PLAY FOR WORK

The above line paraphrases Woody Allen—it's how he directs his movies, and great Power Players know it by heart. Power Players recruit the best people and then they get out of their way. Power Players recruit class and talent and then they shut up. Why recruit the best if you're not going to let them do their thing? Power Players are smart and ego-less enough to allow their stars to step up to the challenge and do their thing. Give talent an unobstructed view. Give them the space and support to show their gifts and win the day. Don't second-guess, don't read over their shoulder and don't stand behind them waiting to catch the ball you think they're about to drop. Get out of their way and shut up.

► THE STORY

My second boss was terrific. He had a lot of trust in me so he got out of my way and let me do my thing. Working together once on a pitch, we had different ideas about the strategy. He deferred to my judgment and backed me up in the room with the clients. We won the business and I had more respect for him that day than on any other. He was and still is a class act.

TOO MUCH PARTNERSHIP MEANS NOT ENOUGH INITIATIVE

POWER PLAY FOR WORK

Power Players are leaders. Though they value partnership and collaboration, they also recognise that too much partnership can mean not enough initiative. The thing about working together in a team is that it can result in you assuming the other person is doing more (so you relax) and your partner in crime assumes the same. As a consequence, the details fall through the cracks and nothing gets done quite the way it should. A successful partnership is a tricky needle to thread. We all need to rely on others in business and it's healthy to collaborate, but there are times when going it alone is the key to success. Power Players keep initiative at the top of their list and work for just the right balance between partnership and playing lone ranger. It's a great skill and only the best Power Players have it.

▶ THE STORY

I do some consulting work for a company and we have weekly training sessions as a team. As much as the sessions are collaborative, it's my job and responsibility to shape and drive those sessions. These guys are looking for a leader and I'm it, which means they need me to set the direction and push them a little to learn more and do better. It works because the content for the sessions is my decision and mine alone. The team members can bring issues to the table and ask for specific issues to be covered, but in the end I need to be responsible for making it happen.

BEND IT, DON'T BREAK IT

POWER PLAY FOR WORK AND PLAY

Power Players know this one by heart. In every situation there's a line that can be walked but never crossed: bend the rules but don't break them. Push the agenda as much as you can but don't ride roughshod all over it. Is it incredibly hard to do? You bet your arse it is. That's why there's a particular art to pushing things just enough to get things done but not so much as to cause a catastrophe. It's in this space between that the great work gets done. The great decisions get made and life becomes victorious.

▶ THE STORY

I watched a Power Player push a writer just that little bit further until a truly wonderful piece of dialogue came out of his mouth and onto the page. The writer was frustrated, bordering on angry, and the Power Player motivated him to greatness. All from bending it but not breaking it.

LEARN WHEN TO STOP

POWER PLAY FOR WORK AND PLAY

It might sound simple, but knowing when to stop is pretty hard to do. Push too far, too fast and whatever it is you're trying to achieve falls off a cliff. Don't push far enough and the whole thing falls short. It's a tricky skill to master and Power Players know exactly when to stop. And the way they learn? They pushed a few things (or people) off a cliff. You've got to get it wrong quite a few times before you know when. It's like driving a manual—you only find that midpoint in your clutch after you've stalled it a few hundred times, but once you've mastered it you rarely stall again. Invest the energy and the time to finding your own 'stop point'. Once you've found it you'll rarely push too far (or not far enough) again.

► THE STORY

I was adamant that I wasn't going to continue to work on a new business concept that was slowly making me crazy, despite being a fantastic idea and as close to a sure thing as possible. A colleague reminded me that the reason it was tough was because no one had pulled it off before and not to give up or I would regret it. Of course, I started to be disagreeable and that's precisely when she stopped pushing. She'd done her job, getting me to think about how dumb it would be to stop when I was ninety-five percent across the finish line. I took a breath, regrouped and didn't give up.

⬆ PLAY FAIR, ESPECIALLY WHEN YOU HAVE THE WINNING CARDS

POWER PLAY FOR WORK

This play is the best way to separate honourable Power Players from the dicks. If you already hold the winning cards, playing fairly is all that's left. A win is a win; there's no need to decimate or humiliate your opponent. If your objective is victory, whatever the project, there can be no joy in watching your opponent fail. Fair play still means something in business even if it is on rare display today. There will be a day sooner than you think when you and your opponent cross paths again. Though they will remember that you won, what they will remember far more is that you played fair. Power Players don't sour a win with unsportsmanlike conduct. Though McEnroe was a great tennis player, the thing we most remember is the guy who screamed at the umpire. Björn Borg was simply great.

► THE STORY

I got my arse kicked by a competitor. We were both pitching our boss an idea for a start-up. He didn't just win—his idea made mine look so amateur that every time I think about it I want to shrivel up and die. Worse, I was the designated 'special person' in the office and management's favourite. Yet he was such a gentleman about it: no rubbing my nose in it, no making me feel like a total failure and no patronising comments about how I should 'keep my chin up'. He won fair and square, and he played fair too.

LOSE THE TRASH-TALK

POWER PLAY FOR LIFE

Power Players keep a very civil tongue. This goes hand in hand with avoiding all malicious or salacious gossip and is much harder than it appears to be. Most of us in the heat of the moment love to sink to trashy levels; we can't help it and, frankly, many of us enjoy it. Mostly we put it down to blowing off some steam but real-life Power Players find other ways to blow off steam, like playing Xbox or taking boxing classes. But seriously, Power Players know that two minutes of trash-talk cancels out all the good and noble stuff that has gone before. Learn from the best and keep a civil tongue, no matter how much it kills you. Leave the room. Take a walk around the block. Just lose the trash-talk, because Forrest Gump said it best: stupid is as stupid does. And trash-talk is stupid.

▸ THE STORY

I went to dinner with a colleague and after one too many he started trash-talking his boss. It was brutal. Even though his boss is a tremendous douche, that is no excuse for trash-talk. The next morning, deeply embarrassed (and slightly hungover), he came into my office and apologised for being so indiscreet. And I'm so glad he restored my faith in him.

BORED MEANS YOU'RE BORING

POWER PLAY FOR THE REST OF YOUR LIFE

Power Players never say 'I'm bored'. Why? Because they firmly believe that people who are bored are actually boring themselves. Power Players are okay with being called a lot of things but boring isn't one of them, because they know that interesting people seek out other interesting people like magnets. Power Players procure a decent percentage of their power from coming across as engaging, often fascinating and sometimes enthralling, but never boring. If you do find that you are bored, take a lead from Power Players and do whatever it takes to makes yourself interesting again. Get a new hobby. Read more. Do something a little unhinged—whatever it takes to feel like life isn't passing you by. Never be in that mental place where people think you're boring.

▶ THE STORY

I was set up on a blind date; why on earth I went I'll never know. Almost the first words out of his mouth were these: 'I get bored really easily.' I had absolutely no idea how to take that. Was he telling me he gets bored with women quickly? Or that he has the attention span of a two-year-old? What? Then it occurred to me: who says that? And then thirty minutes later I realised that he was the most boring man I'd ever met. Boring is as boring does. If you get bored quickly, you just don't have any imagination.

WATCH AND READ POWER

POWER PLAY FOR LIFE

Power Players are suckers for the way benevolent power is portrayed on the big screen and in books. They watch and read as much material as they can get their hands on. Sometimes it really is benevolent, like *The West Wing*'s Josiah Bartlet or *Meet Joe Black*'s William Parrish. Sometimes it's watching the power of *The Godfather*'s Vito Corleone. Or maybe it's Katniss Everdeen from *The Hunger Games* or reading about Winston Churchill or J. Edgar Hoover. Whatever it might be, Power Players like to read and watch how others wear their power. Do they wear it lightly? Are they cruel and unusual? Where do they draw the line? How do they deal with feelings of doubt or self-loathing? Never underestimate the stuff you can learn from simply watching others wear or use their power. Watch, read and observe as much as you can. The world's greatest Power Players always do.

▸ THE STORY

My friend reads biographies of leaders and presidents. He loves to learn all about them and he sees it as the cheapest MBA there is. I always used to think it was hilarious but not anymore. He's right. Learn from those who've gone before. Learn from those around you. Soak it up and watch examples of the power you admire as well as the use of power you reject. Watch and learn.

⬆ LOVE THE OLD-FASHIONED

POWER PLAY FOR ANYWHERE, ANYTIME

We could be talking about the cocktail, but in fact I mean the respect Power Players reserve for old-fashioned stuff that works or is charming. Words like 'cockamamie' or 'hootenanny', that should be revived simply because they sound great. Old-fashioned manners like saying 'sir' or 'ma'am' to the appropriate people need to be brought back into the day-to-day lexicon. Why not? These words are charm personified. Power Players have a terrific sense of history and love to pay homage to the old-fashioned. There's something really classy about it too. Get to love the old-fashioned—it will charm people's socks off. Drop the occasional old-fashioned word or demonstrate your old-fashioned manners and you'll be amazed at the reaction. Power Players know exactly where and when to use their old-fashioned charm. Listen to your instincts and you will too.

▶ THE STORY

A male friend of mine still walks on the curbside when we're strolling down the street. Another always holds the umbrella when we're sharing one. Yet another holds doors open for me. I don't think of any of these actions as sexist but representative of an old-fashioned type of charm. It's good manners and I absolutely love it.

‘IF YOU WANT TO TELL PEOPLE THE TRUTH, MAKE THEM LAUGH . . .’

POWER PLAY FOR LIFE

‘. . . otherwise they’ll kill you.’ Oscar Wilde said it: it was true then and it’s true now. Power Players understand the basic truth that for many if not most of us, the truth is hard to hear. It’s even harder when it’s something so confronting, so awful that we do everything we can to run away from it. Power Players always make people laugh just before telling them a difficult truth. They use humour as the release valve to truth, the elixir required to help the recipient of said truth face the music. Every time you need to tell an uncomfortable truth, pre-empt with humour—a joke, a good story—anything that will make them laugh. No matter how bad the truth, invariably there are worse things in the world, and humour has a terrific way of delivering some much-needed perspective.

► THE STORY

My sister and I were guests at a New Year’s Eve ball that was filled with a bunch of very strange people who could have passed for the cast of *The Rocky Horror Picture Show*. One very drunk man sidled up to my sister and tried to pick her up. She turned to him as deadpan as possible and said ‘You had me at hello.’ He laughed uproariously, at which point my sister gently pointed out that he was drunk and touching her leg and he should step away before things got nasty. He walked away and we got the hell out of there. Humour to diffuse, immediately followed by the truth. Funny and effective.

IMAGINATION IS PURE GOLD

POWER PLAY FOR WORK

Albert Einstein said that 'The true sign of intelligence is not knowledge but imagination', and he was one smart bloke. Power Players always have a healthy respect for knowledge but they also know that imagination is the true gold. We can all learn and read and study, but the sign of real, undisputed intelligence is imagination. Having the ability to conjure up a new idea by throwing something out to the universe that is original, exciting and smacks of newness is not only incredibly alluring but also shows a great mind at work. Power Players do everything they can to enable and encourage their imagination. Mental gymnastics, crazy ideas, connecting the mental dots—anything and everything that allows the imagination to flourish. Look for people who have an active and fertile imagination, and choose to have these people in your inner circle because knowledge can be taught but imagination is innate.

▸ THE STORY

My business partner has an incredibly fertile imagination. When we started developing our Cupcakes Delivered online business, he came up with these fantastic sticks that would stop our cakes from wiggling around in the box, thereby allowing these cupcakes to be couriered anywhere in Australia and arrive undamaged. Great imagination, plus that's money in the bank.

➊ 'EVERY SAINT HAS A PAST AND EVERY SINNER HAS A FUTURE'

POWER PLAY FOR EVERY PART OF YOUR LIFE

Another Oscar Wilde gem. Nothing is static, including people. Each of us has a past, and a future that has yet to unfold. For some of us, our best days are behind us. If you're anything like me, you're hopeful that your best days are ahead of you. People who are good today may be that way because of a sordid past. A person who is bad today always has the chance to be a better person tomorrow, so don't be too quick to judge. When it comes to people, Power Players try to see the whole picture. Rarely is a person black or white—there are saints and sinners in all of us. Anyone who appears saintly you can surely bet has some skeletons in the closet, and anyone who comes across as a bad person is probably capable of real decency. Remember this before you brand someone good or bad. None of us is entirely one or the other.

▶ THE STORY

I made a new friend and thought she was terrific. Smart, funny, kind and decent, she was a volunteer for a local charity and seemed to have her life together more than most. Many months into our friendship she told me her story. She'd been a drug addict and spent some time in jail. She'd also turned to prostitution to support her habit. I was a little stunned to say the least and wondered whether we'd be friends now if I'd known all that when I met her. Judgment has a funny way of shaping our choices and decisions. We've all done stuff we wish we could undo, and some histories are worse than others. Don't judge.

PREDICTABILITY CAN BE UNINSPIRED

POWER PLAY FOR WORK

Power Players never really warm to people who love the concept of predictability. They rate this word right up there with dull, mediocre, unimaginative and lacklustre. Predictability absolutely has its place, but top-notch Power Players understand that it can act as an obstacle to genius. They also know it's a comfortable word that can temper the desire (and need) for energy and brilliance and momentum. Don't misunderstand: predictability is of course better than total unpredictability or, worse, chaos. The point of this Power Play is that consistency is something we all tend to hide behind from time to time; because we're 'predictable' we don't need to be more than that, we trick ourselves into thinking that it's enough. The thing is, the great stuff usually comes from more than predictability. It comes from inspiration, it comes from magic, it comes from a surge of energy and creativity that flies in the face of predictability. Understand the difference between the two. The most impressive Power Players always do.

► THE STORY

I worked with a guy who was so damned consistent he'd make exactly the same speech to every single client about the importance of having 'a social media strategy'. In fact, he was so consistent about this point that he gave the speech twice to the same client and the client finished his sentence for him. After a while we used to mouth the words of his stories behind his back because he'd crossed over from consistent to predictable. The next step from there is to be irrelevant. And the only thing worse than being hated is being called irrelevant.

PLANT THE SEED, THEN WALK AWAY

POWER PLAY FOR WORK

Power Players are fantastic seed-planters. They give up just enough information to gently suggest a direction while still making it look like the direction is entirely the other person's choice. Power Players know that most of us are simply looking for a stepping-off point, and once we get that from the people we trust we can absolutely take it from there. There is a particular skill to planting a seed: a few perfectly selected words followed by a pause are then underlined with a mini-gauntlet being thrown down. Then you walk away. Quietly. But this tactic only works if you know exactly what to say and which chord to strike. Get it wrong and the seed becomes a stink bomb, and then the whole thing goes to hell in a handbasket. The best Power Players can conjure up magic with just a few choice words, and when you see it happen right in front of you it really is sublime. Learn this one as quickly as you can. It will be a trademark move for you.

▸ THE STORY

A guy who worked for me used to go round and round in circles when trying to headline a great idea. He was fantastic at coming up with top ideas but terrible at selling them; he always buried the lead. I would watch him pace and practise presenting the idea, then to get him back on track I'd simply suggest a sentence to start. I'd take his own words and rearrange them for him. And because he was a billion times smarter than me, that was all it took. Plant seeds and let them grow.

MAKE TIME FOR COFFEE

POWER PLAY FOR LIFE

Power Players always make time to get people away from the office for a terrific cup of coffee. Getting away allows people to let their guards down and be themselves rather than some version of who they think they should be. With no set agenda, Power Players do the coffee thing as often as they can and see where the conversation goes. Always make time for coffee. Take your guest out, get them that double shot skim latte or whatever they like, sit back and let them spill. Because you're not the one who does the talking, they are. Power Players use these coffee catch-ups to listen to whatever is going on in the person's head. Even when things get busy, Power Players don't nix the coffee break from their schedule.

▶ THE STORY

For a while I got a little stingy with my time and pulled the plug on all the coffees I kept getting asked to. Pretty soon the good ideas stopped popping into my head. Putting people together with other people who could really help each other professionally stopped too. And then I realised it was because I'd pulled the plug on all the coffees. Grabbing a coffee with people opens them up. Relaxed and often at their best, random conversations happen and connections are made, both literally and intellectually. Don't get stingy with the coffees.

VISIT YOUR HISTORY

POWER PLAY FOR LIFE

Power Players like to take a good look at where they've come from. It helps them keep their perspective. Visiting their history is one of the best ways to get a view of the future and where things might go. Go visit your history from time to time. See where you've come from when things were (or at least seemed) simpler. Taking the occasional trip down memory lane is clarifying, illuminating and sometimes even exhilarating to Power Players. Make sure you remember your history. Don't ever bury your history or, worse, try to rewrite it. Embrace it, visit it and most of all learn from it.

▶ THE STORY

I grew up in St Marys in the far western suburbs of Sydney. It was a tough neighbourhood and some of the kids I went to school with ended up in jail on serious offences. My first boss told me that I should 'bury' where I grew up, but I disagreed. It was the best place in the world I could have grown up. It's real life and it set me straight on a lot of things. More than that, the people who live in St Marys have more character and dignity than a lot of people I've met in the grown-up business world. I hope I haven't patronised St Marys and its people because I'm proud of the place. Don't bury your history. No matter how good or bad, it's still your own.

WHEN YOU'RE BROKEN, GET PATCHED UP PROPERLY

POWER PLAY FOR LIFE

Power Players make sure they get put back together, just like Rocky Balboa. When they have a terrible run and they're all smashed up, they stop and get revived. They don't pretend they're okay or 'soldier on'. They take themselves out of the game and they heal. This is perhaps one of the most important lessons you'll ever learn from the genuine article, a fully-fledged Power Player. If you're not at your best, you need to have the guts to take yourself out of the game. Two weeks of rest is better than a year of being a bird with a clipped wing. It takes great strength to admit that you need time to get patched up properly. And once you take that time, you'll be better and stronger and smarter than ever. Now that's real power.

▶ THE STORY

I could write a whole new book about the broken stuff. Not gonna. You've got your sad song, so when you're all messed up, play it and take yourself out of the game.

PICK YOUR THEME SONG

POWER PLAY FOR LIFE

The world's greatest Power Players have their own theme song. I have one. So should you. You can play it on your iPhone or just play it in your head. Whatever, as long as you play it when you need it most. Music can change your entire mood. It bolsters confidence, makes you feel like you have an edge, gives you the secret ingredient to your success and, most of all, it's cool. Find your theme song, something you'll never tire of and something you truly love. Whenever you feel shaky or fragile or just plain crappy, play it. It will do the trick every time, and other Power Players will recognise that strut immediately.

▶ THE STORY

Who'd have thought it? I have my own theme song especially for days when I'm not feeling so great. I crank it as soon as I have woken and I dance around the house in my pyjamas. I pretend I'm a star on Broadway and strut until I start to feel like I'm shaking the bad vibe loose. I couldn't care less who sees me and it always stops any dark cloud from settling over my head. Get a song and get it now. It works.

ALWAYS ASSUME THEY'RE SMARTER THAN YOU ARE

POWER PLAY FOR WORK

Power Players usually assume they're the dumbest player in the room. Why? It's safer than thinking they're the smartest. If you take this basic premise as a start point, you're covered. Why do Power Players do this? Because it motivates them (forces them, actually) to make absolutely sure that they are prepared. More likely over-prepared. The added bonus is that it stops them from being arrogant and superior. Humility when it comes to talent is a Power Player trademark move. Worrying whether you're good enough makes you become good enough—usually great enough. The minute you enter a room thinking you're top dog you can be assured the whole thing will get blown to high heaven. Assume they're smart, then you'll be smarter.

► THE STORY

I was meeting with some really smart people who basically own the wedding industry, and I knew for sure I'd be the dumbest person in the room. I studied for every possible question that might be asked. I got somebody who works in the industry to give me a crash course in all things bridal and wedding. After the crash course I realised I knew even less than I thought. And I went back and studied some more.

⬆ JUST SHUT UP AND GO TO CHURCH

POWER PLAY FOR LIFE

Power Players shut up and go to church with their mothers, even if they don't believe in the Almighty and even if they feel a little bit weird about it. They do this because sometimes you just need to stop thinking about your needs and start thinking about the other person's. I take my mother to church and so should you (that's if she wants to go, of course). This is a parable about Power Players sometimes having to do things they'd rather not. Don't lecture, don't cajole and don't force your POV on others. Sometimes the right thing to do is to go along to get along. This isn't a sign of weakness—it's actually a sign of strength. Holding your tongue and showing supreme grace is one of the most elegant trademark Power Player moves you can ever do.

▶ THE STORY

I know nothing about golf. I don't want to know anything about golf. I don't even think it's a sport. It's walking. But every few months I play golf with a colleague and friend of mine because he loves golf and I love him. I always have a great time with him and it opens me up to the possibility of one day learning to have a healthy respect for golf. It's a simple decision to go and I just shut up and do it. I'm not sure my friend even knows I hate golf (though maybe my praying for rain last time gave me away).

A FLAME-OUT CAN MEAN ONLY ONE THING: A COMEBACK

POWER PLAY FOR EVERY PART OF YOUR LIFE

When Power Players go down in flames, they don't muck around. If it all goes south in a big and public way, they wallow for a while (privately), regroup and then do what Power Players do best: they make a big, huge, splashy comeback. The best thing about flaming out is that a smashing Hollywood comeback is just around the corner. It's easy to like someone when they're on top. The true measure of a person is seeing how they react when things are otherwise. Power Players don't wander off into the wilderness to die like dogs: they regroup (maybe after a bottle of good scotch) and then make their comeback. A quintessential Power Player move.

▶ THE STORY

A friend of mine sent an ill-advised email to a client in the heat of the moment. The email was completely and totally out of line. My friend lost his job, lost a lawsuit and lost his girlfriend. Not a great day's work. He drank for a month, smoked cigarettes for breakfast for a month and slept until midday for a month. Then he apologised to the client and slowly started putting his life back together. In job interviews, my friend was honest and direct: 'I screwed up and I screwed up huge. It cost me my whole life and all the money in my bank account and I won't be doing that again.' He now lives in Los Angeles and runs a major movie studio. There's always room for a comeback.

⬆ READ *TO KILL A MOCKINGBIRD* . . . AGAIN

POWER PLAY FOR LIFE

The world's greatest Power Players have a copy of Harper Lee's *To Kill a Mockingbird* on their bedside table. There is no greater hero than Atticus Finch and no greater siblings than Scout and Jem. It's hard to keep one's moral compass in a world where morals are bent all the time and doing the right thing sounds great on paper but rarely happens in real life. Reading *To Kill a Mockingbird* will set you straight again in lightning speed. You'll gather some courage and wish you *were* Atticus Finch. We all need a novel that makes us feel heroic, inspires us to be better and do better, and lifts us out of a trough when we're feeling pathetic and our confidence is less than zero. Find your book and make it your bible. Read it when you need inspiration—read it once a month if you have to. Power Players have their book. Pick yours.

▶ THE STORY

Just read a book that speaks to you again and again. And again.

ANYONE CAN GET TO ANYONE

POWER PLAY FOR WORK

Power Players have a unique view of opportunity and destiny: if somebody is more accomplished, higher up the food chain or tough to get to, they don't rule out a meeting. If it's important for them to make contact with that person, they find a way to make it happen. They see it as a thrilling challenge. To Power Players, anyone can get to anyone, but the cool factor is how they go about it. They don't pander or grovel or stalk—they simply find a clever way to get to their intended target. Take a big lead from Power Players: they are fearless when it comes to meeting the people who will make a difference to their professional life. They are authentic and honest and often endearing, and this lets them get exactly what they want: an introduction. Be fearless when it comes to making a new introduction. You'll be amazed at how well it works.

▸ THE STORY

My first business partner picked up the phone, called Virgin and got a meeting with Richard Branson, smooth-talking his way in. He then got on a plane and went to see him with an idea. The idea become a joint venture deal between Optus and Virgin Mobile, and the rest is the rest.

⬆ POSITIVE IMPACT—THAT'S REAL POWER

POWER PLAY FOR LIFE

When Power Players flex their power muscles, the impact and impression they leave is positive. Often it's more than positive: it's joyful. Their definition of power is something to be used for good. The hidden charm of this is that it fosters an enormous amount of goodwill amongst people, so when Power Players make a grand decision or big move, the people around them are more likely to trust in their judgment. This is the payoff of positive power. It doesn't come with a lot of suspicion and resistance—it comes with blind faith and lots of action. Think about the men and women who've practised positive power: JFK, Martin Luther King, Oprah Winfrey . . . People trust them and tend to leave their cynicism at the door. It's a fantastic lesson. Learn from it.

▶ THE STORY

My favourite Power Player in the world is incapable of making a single move that doesn't benefit at least a dozen people. He looks at creating a start-up and involves a bunch of people whose lives are immediately richer. The mood is positive, the idea is usually fantastic, and the energy is infectious. It's all a positive, rewarding experience. It's unbelievable to watch, and even more unbelievable to be a part of.

NEED FOR NOTHING

POWER PLAY FOR LIFE

When push comes to shove, Power Players can be a neat little self-contained unit if they need to be. No accolades, no hero-worship, no pity party. This in turn makes them incredibly powerful. Being self-contained requires very little expenditure of false energy, the kind where you constantly worry about what you're not getting, what people aren't saying, the accolades you aren't receiving. Power Players learn to love the small acts of kindness and happiness in life. If they lose the big job and the perks that come with it, they can go back to living a lean and simple life. As soon as the money starts to roll, take a big lead from Power Players: get into the habit of needing for nothing. It will make you more powerful than you can possibly imagine.

▶ THE STORY

My dearest friend, a Power Player in the banking industry, could walk away from it all tomorrow and be perfectly happy. He loves his job and is brilliant at it, but his job is not who he is—it's what he does. He doesn't need a lot of attention or recognition. His self-containment makes him pretty unusual—extraordinary even.

MAKE PEACE WITH UNCERTAINTY

POWER PLAY FOR LIFE

The world's greatest Power Players make living with uncertainty a fine art. The best ones even throw in a little extra uncertainty from time to time to remember that chaos could be just around the corner and that there is beauty in messiness. Power Players also know that when things are going great, you can bet good money that it's all about to go to hell. They are very, very good at keeping a level head when they are having a dream run. More importantly, they also know that the best ideas come in times of uncertainty, but this can only happen if you can make peace with uncertainty. And when you can look uncertainty dead in the eye without flinching, you're the genuine power-playing article.

▶ THE STORY

A hero of mine has spent the last fifteen years of her life in total uncertainty. A debilitating illness means she is at the mercy of prescribed drugs and the way her body responds to them. She is also a writer of stories for small-circulation magazines while trying to get her first novel published; it doesn't pay much, but enough for her to get by. Her illness is degenerative, so in the next ten years she will lose her ability to care for herself. Yet amidst all this uncertainty, she gets up at seven every morning, writes until midday, goes about her chores for a couple of hours in the afternoon and starts writing again from two until five in the afternoon. She is disciplined and motivated when most other people I know would probably give up the game completely. Talk about making peace with uncertainty.

THE PROOF OF GREATNESS: ENDURE CRITICISM WITHOUT RESENTMENT

POWER PLAY FOR WORK, PLAY AND LOVE

Elbert Hubbard said something along those lines—and how true it is! You can count on one hand the number of people who can take the heat and not retaliate. When most of us are faced with criticism of any kind, our first reaction is to lash out. Few of us take a breath, see if the criticism is warranted (which it often is), take our medicine and replace hubris with humility.

▶ THE STORY

Of all the Power Players I look up to, the one I admire the most is a guy who screwed up and screwed up huge. He got wildly drunk at a work function and started performing a striptease. He was set straight by the global CEO who did not mince words and was absolutely justified in doing so. The Power Player knew he was wrong, so he kept his head down, apologised to the people who deserved an apology and changed his ways. He never exhibited that behaviour again and, moreover, he never resented the criticism. A good man, if you ask me, and exactly the reaction that proves greatness.

BE WORTHY OF TRUST

POWER PLAY FOR WORK, PLAY, LIFE, LOVE

Power Players don't use big words unless they understand their meaning. Trust is one of those big words. Power Players know that trust is hard to build and must be earned. They also know that if trust is broken it is almost impossible to rebuild. Power Players don't expect to be trusted by their team simply because they happen to be in a position of power; if anything, they know this generally makes people more suspicious and less likely to trust. The truly awesome Power Players earn their trust step by little step. They demonstrate their decency and character and show that their word is their bond. There is no other way to earn real trust. Your job as a Power Player is to be worthy of it.

▸ THE STORY

I took my crew out to a Christmas dinner where things got out of hand pretty quickly. By the end of the night, the owner of the restaurant told me he was nervous and it needed to stop or he'd have to call the police. I rounded up the crew, told them to rein it in and set them loose on the city. By all accounts they were fine. On Monday morning, my boss called me into his office, having heard about the Friday night behaviour. He asked me exactly what went on and I told him that everybody had just blown off some steam and that I'd already sent a hamper and movie tickets for the restaurant owner. Case closed. My crew sat sheepishly waiting for me to come out of the boss's office. I told them that they were safe, but that was their one get-out-of-jail-free card. If they can't trust me, I'm no use to them. And they never let things get out of control again.

⬆ WINNERS ALWAYS WANT THE BALL

POWER PLAY FOR WORK

Power Players like to be winners. They love to get the job done. The thing about winning, though, is that you need to put yourself in the best position for success. There's the old sports adage: winners always want the ball. And Power Players never run away when the ball comes their way. You can always tell a failed Power Player: they run away when the ball is thrown in their direction. If you really want to graduate to Power Player status, you've got to get in the game. And when that ball comes your way, you have to run with it and score the winning shot. These may be cheesy sport metaphors, but they make an incredibly important point about being front and centre when the game is being played and the ball comes your way.

▶ THE STORY

An intern I grew to love lived this philosophy. Every time there was writing to be done on a pitch document, she would volunteer her services and put herself in the line of fire, doing the job of someone with ten years more experience. She would take a first crack, hand it to me for corrections and rewrites and then get them done. She would volunteer for all the jobs that put her in the spotlight, for better or worse. Gutsy stuff. She is now running a division of a broadcast company in the United States and is the youngest person they've ever had in that position. All because winners want the ball.

DON'T TRASH THE TRASHY

POWER PLAY FOR LIFE

We all come across trashy types who have very little class, not much character and only a fraction of decency. These people are easy targets—which is exactly the reason Power Players leave them alone. Don't pick on people because you think you can. If they're trashy, they've got enough problems already. It's a low and inelegant blow to go after the weakest amongst us. Power Players never pick on weaklings and always fight fair. If you pick on someone who has their own crap going on, you'll never recover. It's the kidney punch of business and it's low-rent all the way.

▶ THE STORY

When my best friend split up with her boyfriend he soon after moved on to another girl. We all found ourselves at the same party many months later where my friend had to undergo the classic introduction to the new girlfriend. She was polite, charming and warm to her; in her situation I probably would have been apoplectic. The new girlfriend was a bottle blonde, wearing a nightclub outfit with matching glitter stilettos to a casual summer backyard party. As the rest of us stood around in our shorts and t-shirts, she looked like a Vegas hooker. To this day my friend has not said one negative or unkind word about the new girlfriend, despite our baiting. We were low-rent and she was class all the way.

MOJO MAKEOVER

POWER PLAY FOR LIFE

From time to time, everybody loses his or her mojo. You know the feeling: you can't do anything right, everything you touch turns to failure and it's as if bad luck follows you around wherever you go. When you feel you're on a downward spiral you have to arrest this spiral in its tracks: what you need is a mojo makeover. Power Players know that bad luck is a self-fulfilling prophecy and are genius at stopping their sinking mojo in its tracks. In order to turn bad luck around they need to look it in the face and change their mojo. A spate of negative stuff will only stay negative if you believe you're due even more bad luck. If you think you're due a break, good stuff will start to happen again. Be shamelessly positive and the good luck will slowly start to flow again.

▶ THE STORY

I tend to gravitate toward superstitious people. For some reason I like them. This guy I know well felt that his mojo had been forever altered, so he decided to fly in the face of it and shake the demons away. On a freezing cold day in the middle of winter, with torrential rain bucketing down, he decided to go for a run and then a swim in the ocean. Everyone around him was falling down with flu so he decided he would tempt the flu gods. Not only did he not get sick, but he also then decided to buy a lottery ticket. He won five hundred bucks and the bad mojo was banished for good. Fly in the face of it. It really does work.

NEVER FORFEIT YOUR RIGHT TO FIGHT

POWER PLAY FOR WORK AND RELATIONSHIPS

Power Players always reserve the right to fight. Yes, the sentiment may rhyme, but it's more than just poetic. If something is totally dumb or just plain wrong, Power Players fight the injustice. Gentle and subtle are always preferable ways to go, but if what's required is a nice, juicy knockdown, then so be it. Think about the scene in *The Godfather* where Clemenza tells Michael Corleone that every few years a good messy feud between the Mafia heads is exactly the ticket: clears out the bad blood. Sometimes a good old-fashioned brawl in business achieves what no amount of pussyfooting behaviour can deliver. Suit up and fight (when you have to). Sometimes it really is the best course of action.

▶ THE STORY

My sister and I went through a pretty rough patch. Brutal would be a more accurate assessment. It was very hard for us because we have always been incredibly close, closer than most sisters I know. For a while there had been tension but it was unspoken, and it wasn't until we had a knockdown fight that we finally got to the stuff that needed to come out. Only then could we start talking again like real sisters. It wasn't just a small fight—it was epic, fifteen-rounds stuff, but necessary. We've never been closer and we've never been more real with each other. A big fight can be just the tonic to clear away the detritus and start clean.

⬆ GIVE NO TRUCK TO A PUNY ENEMY

POWER PLAY FOR WORK

Power Players don't let the puny enemies steal away their time and attention. They know better than to let the annoying people cause death by a thousand paper cuts. Give no mental real estate to the people who are small in every sense of the word. They can be very dangerous because they are often exhausting and have a way of seeping into your consciousness without you even knowing it, so Power Players are careful to shield themselves from these dangerous types. They do this because they learn to recognise that it's these seemingly harmless ones who can cause the biggest problems. Power Players identify the puny ones fast and then quickly decide to leave them alone.

▶ THE STORY

I worked with someone who used to complain about the font I used in my emails. They didn't like it. Now, my emails would usually contain critical information on pitching business, on clients and opportunities for the company. Who cares about the font? A puny person complaining about a thoroughly unimportant issue.

↑ GUARD YOUR REPUTATION WITH YOUR LIFE

POWER PLAY FOR EVERY MINUTE OF EVERY DAY

Though Power Players don't dwell on how they are perceived by the outside world, they do guard their reputations with their life. What takes a lifetime to create takes a day to destroy. The thing is, though, they focus on doing good work and let the reputation take care of itself. See your reputation the way a Power Player does. It will be built if you do the right thing: work hard, be faithful and fair, and do your best never to cut the wrong corners. Reputation is a strange and delicate beast. All of the very best reputations are built one small accomplishment at a time. But remember this most of all: good works are only a small part of the equation. Good character and kindness make up the better part of reputation.

▶ THE STORY

My boss was unsure of what to do about a couple of guys who'd left to start their own business and had taken a big client with them. My boss had already developed a bit of a reputation for holding grudges so he decided to go the other way: he bought them a bottle of champagne and wished them well, no lawsuit and no fight. So began his reputation as a calm and collected leader. Eighteen months later the guys came back to the CEO and asked to return, with a swag of clients in tow.

TOMORROW IS A NEW DAY

POWER PLAY FOR LIFE

Power Players (like the rest of us) can have particularly crappy days, the kind where you contemplate running away to Jamaica and getting a gig behind a bar. Rather than overreact and lose their heads, Power Players wallow in the awfulness of the day, get a good night's sleep and wake up to a fresh start. There is always a bright, shiny new day tomorrow and Power Players treat each day like a chance for redemption. Hokey, maybe, but it's an excellent lesson to take from Power Players. The very best ones have a unique way of wiping the slate clean after a bad day and giving the new day everything they've got. For every shitty day, there's a good one just around the corner. It's the law of averages.

▶ THE STORY

One of my favourite Power Players used to look into my face when we were having a particularly bad day and say, 'Tomorrow, Rose, is a new day. Giddy up.' Giddy up indeed. I just love the simplicity of that sentiment!

KNOW WHAT YOU WANT

POWER PLAY FOR LIFE

Once a lovely Power Player asked me a very simple question: 'Do you know what you want?' The way she said it as she eyeballed me stopped me in my tracks. She told me that very few people know what they really, truly want and even fewer can articulate it in one simple sentence. Power Players almost always know what they want. They are resolute, secure in the knowledge that because they know exactly what they want, they can create some type of a solid plan to get there. Always ask yourself what you want (this is the hard part). Once you've worked this out, the way to get there tends to slowly formulate. Ask yourself with regularity exactly what it is you want; you'll be amazed at what falls out of your mouth.

▶ THE STORY

My girlfriend has spent half her life building her career. She thought it was exactly what she wanted until she found out it wasn't: what she wanted was to become a mum. Deep down it's all she's ever wanted, and in this age of 'empowered women' she felt she was betraying the sisterhood. But she decided to go after what she wanted. She found a lovely man, got married and had four children in quick succession. I've never seen her happier. She is living her dream out loud and is one of the greatest mums I've ever seen. Know what you want and go get it.

BE AN ELITIST

POWER PLAY FOR WORK

Power Players don't apologise for having an elitist point of view. This shouldn't be mistaken for snobbery or arrogance but for a desire to hold true to the qualities in life that have (sadly, I think) become unpopular. These qualities include deference to intellect, to scholarship, to striving for the very, very best a person can achieve. Power Players know that it's good to be ambitious and that admiring great minds and great thinkers moves a society forward. Some people ridicule big brains and big ideas. Power Players don't belong in this category. They embrace the readers, the seekers and the challengers, the people who love a good, respectful argument. Exercise your mind. Reach for better. Power Players always do.

▶ THE STORY

A journalist friend of mine bemoans the death of good writing and quality journalism. He hates the way everything is being 'dumbed down'. Every time he finds himself in a room with (what he calls) lowest common denominator people building a case for dumb stories, he argues the case for smarter stories that force readers to flex their intellectual muscles. He never wins these arguments, but it doesn't stop him from trying. Somebody has to fight the good fight.

LET IT FALL APART

POWER PLAY FOR WORK

Power Players know when to let it all fall apart. Sometimes the best course of action is to let something die a natural death, whether it is a bad idea, a dumb strategy or clumsily assembled plans. The reason Power Players sometimes let it all fall apart is that building something new is far better than doing a patch-up job on something that sits on a shaky foundation. If it isn't solid and real, better to let it all come down, then you can build all over again. This is an incredibly valuable lesson to learn from shrewd Power Players: if it isn't working, let it go and let the dust settle before building anew.

▶ THE STORY

A guy I love more than life itself is fantastic at letting things fall apart. We were once writing a pitch document together and we'd spent maybe twenty hours on it. He'd done the lion's share of the writing and it was time to print and review the work. The writing was not good. Most people would have tried to patch it up or make peace with the bad writing but not him. In a grand and dramatic gesture, he tore it all up into little pieces, threw the pieces on the floor and turned to me to say, 'I can do so much better and so can you. We're starting again!' Love it.

EMBRACE FIDELITY

POWER PLAY FOR EVERY SINGLE DAY

This one isn't about marriage vows (though I'm a fan), it's about being true to the commitments you've made in business. If you say you're going to do it, do it—no if, ands or buts. Or don't make the promise in the first place. Power Players absolutely hate breaking promises, even if it's as small as picking up a coffee for a colleague on the way to the office or calling somebody back by the time they said they would. Fidelity means being faithful to your word, and most of us can count on one hand the people who live by this principle. No matter how big (or indeed small) the promise you make, be faithful to that promise. Be faithful in all the things you undertake and make fidelity a new-fashioned word.

▶ THE STORY

I promised a client five great ideas within twenty-four hours on a big problem they were having. It was Friday afternoon at four, so the ideas were due by Saturday at four. Even though it was the weekend and the client might not check his emails, it didn't matter. I'd said twenty-four hours and that was now the ballgame. The ideas were great: imaginative, well articulated and brought to life visually. We got the ideas in a few hours early and at one in the afternoon the client replied saying he loved them. We won his respect for sticking to our word and not blowing our deadline out to Monday. Fidelity matters.

⬆ ECCENTRIC ISN'T A DIRTY WORD

POWER PLAY FOR LIFE

Power Players embrace eccentricity and the people who exhibit these fantastic qualities. Why? Because the long and short of it is this: eccentricity suggests the ability to see the world through unique eyes, and that level of originality is priceless. To a lot of people, eccentric is a dirty word. It's like calling someone 'interesting', which is code for crazy and unlikeable. Unlike most of us, eccentrics don't try to belong to a clique or tribe or group because they've made peace with the reality that they never will. Power Players seek out the eccentrics and bring them into their world. Being a little bit odd, unconventional and unlike others in the room is a precious gift, and Power Players see it this way. They don't run from strange and they don't surround themselves with conventional and predictable. If you're smart, you'll follow suit.

▶ THE STORY

Being the lifelong holder of a minority opinion, my head tends to start in a different place to everybody else's, for better or worse. An airline client once asked me to 'use my crazy head' to come up with a whole new way of carving up the classes on a plane, so I did. We played around with the idea of creating planes that were purpose-built for people going away on a holiday, or for executives, or for families where their kids could (figuratively) climbs the walls. This led me to thinking about all the things you could do to the space inside the plane if first, business and cattle class were removed and new designations put in. It might put the fun back into flying and even allow the airline to charge for all sorts of things they could never have gotten away with before. If you immediately see things differently, embrace it. Good stuff comes from this place.

BE A ROMANTIC

POWER PLAY FOR WORK, LIFE AND LOVE

Believing in romance and being a fan of the grand romantic gesture brings a whole lot of hope to a seemingly hopeless world. This Power Play isn't about literal romance: it's about believing that there can be a happy ending. There are ideas and opportunities and business deals that against all the odds can actually work out perfectly. The best Power Players I know are at heart hopeless romantics. They believe in rainbows after a thunderstorm and perfect endings to complicated (and random) business opportunities. When it comes to business, there's no reason why everything can't proceed perfectly and turn out spectacularly—it can and does happen. Be a romantic. Believe in rainbows. Believe in happy endings. Power Players always make sure that a part of their soul always does.

▶ THE STORY

My business partner and I launched a business that can deliver you a cupcake pretty much anywhere in Australia in twenty-four hours. It's a simple idea yet it was incredibly hard to pull off. We hit roadblock after roadblock, and several times I voted we walk away. My business partner (the eternal optimist and romantic) never allowed me to stop believing in that happy ending. He does believe, and it's sort of miraculous to watch. His crazy, happy-ending belief kept me going, and if the business works (as I suspect it will) it will be because my business partner is a romantic.

THE GLASS IS HALF THE DRINK

POWER PLAY FOR LIFE

I heard this thoroughly fantastic saying from a Power Player at a bar one night as he protested a martini being poured into a test tube rather than the classic martini glass. I asked him why and he turned to me and said with gravitas in his voice, 'The glass is half the drink.' It is one of the best pieces of wisdom I have ever heard. When Power Players get busy planning, they never forget that half the job is the anticipation and pitch theatre that comes with unveiling the big plan. Dressing it up isn't a phony tactic; we can all do with a little bit of drama, fantasy and romance from time to time, and never more so than in the throes of a long business day. The glass is half the drink: what a great saying! It just made it to the top of my list.

▶ THE STORY

I sometimes do training with strategists coming up through the ranks. If we are rehearsing for a big presentation, I make everybody stand up and do it for real, dressed in what they would normally wear and bringing along whatever pitch theatre they need to enhance their performance. If this means big pictures and illustrations to bring their story to life, so be it. If this means displaying the physical product they are selling and how it is used, fine. Once one of the trainees was pitching a tequila drink and she lined up shots for everyone in the room to down. It was one o'clock in the afternoon on a Tuesday and the whole pitch was about proving how crazy and in the moment you feel when you down a shot of tequila. We all felt free that day (some freer that most).

TRUST SLOWLY

POWER PLAY FOR LIFE

Fast friends: even faster enemies. Power Players know this one by heart. That's why they tread slowly when deciding if somebody is completely and wholly trustworthy. It takes time to size up a person, which is a good thing. Trust is a precious and rare connection to build and it's nice to know that once it's been established you can count on it. The world is fast and most of us have lost the art of doing things slowly. If we don't like somebody immediately, we tend to write the person off. Power Players know that some of the best friendships happen slowly, and the very best business partnerships are the ones that turn into friendships as well.

▶ THE STORY

My cupcakes business partner and I knew each other for four years before we started to open up about the personal stuff. It might seem like a long time, but if we're planning on knowing each other for the rest of our lives, four years is a drop in the ocean. Our slow-burn friendship is exhilarating in its own way. It's a bit like slow food: a delicious feast in this fast-food world. Go slow. It's okay.

STOP WHEN THINGS ARE GETTING ENTIRELY TOO SERIOUS

POWER PLAY FOR WORK, PLAY AND LOVE

Power Players know that serious problems need serious people to solve them. But they also know that being heavy on the serious can very quickly result in a person losing their perspective in its entirety. Recently, I was headed in that direction—until I remembered a line from a Power Player I respect more than anything: 'Do something crazy when things are becoming entirely too serious!' This is very, very good advice. There's something about seriousness that acts as a type of negative force, and bad things happen when there's an overdose of it. The minute it's all you can see and feel, break the serious jinx and mix it up—a joke, something nuts, anything to shake off the serious.

▸ THE STORY

I can't even type a serious story because even that's entirely too serious! You know it when you need to drop the serious. We all do.

STOP TALKING BEFORE YOU REACH FOR THE TRAPDOOR

POWER PLAY FOR WORK

Power Players have two things going on in their heads when they are talking: they know what they have to say and when they've said it enough. Most of us start looking for the trapdoor through which to fall at the exact moment we've made a verbal boo-boo. It's much easier to say a little less than to spend the next month of your life apologising for some boneheaded remark. Of all the Power Plays, this is perhaps *the* hardest one to do. Most of us love to hear ourselves talk and most of us usually overtalk. If you can train yourself to be economical with language, you'll be way ahead in the verbal gaffe stakes. And it's almost always impossible to un-ring a bell or un-say something stupid or hurtful. Save yourself the pain and humiliation by slowing down before you open up your big mouth.

▶ THE STORY

I was in a meeting and the client was starting to push my buttons. I promised something I shouldn't have—and wouldn't have, if I'd simply stopped talking. The promise cost us money and me my self-respect.

BE GREAT AT DESCRIPTION

POWER PLAY FOR WORK

Power Players are great at painting a mental picture. They love words, and the best Players use words that can unlock even the dullest of imaginations. Fall in love with words and make them your greatest asset; it's much easier to grease the wheels of business when you can tantalise your team's or client's imagination. The coolest Power Players don't reach for the obvious. When they feel bent out of shape they say they're 'discombobulated'. When they think someone is behaving strangely they tell them they are 'unglued'. When they think someone has made a weird call they ask them if they've 'eaten a plate of crazy' for breakfast. They have fun with words. They find new ones to use and they continually expand their vocabulary. Follow the lead of the most entertaining Power Players. Be known for your fantastic descriptions.

▶ THE STORY

I sat in a meeting with a journalist I adore whose command of language is breathtaking. The sentence he used in describing the emotions that come with unrequited love will stay with me until the day I die: 'When the object of your affection rejects you, every ounce of hope and energy and softness and goodwill and tenderness and glory drains from your body. It's as though someone has taken a can opener to your chest and scooped out your heart with a ladle. Your insides are no longer your own and you wonder if you will ever take a shower and brush your teeth and dress yourself and leave your house again.' Wow!

↑ 'IT TAKES A GREAT PERSON TO BE A GOOD LISTENER'

POWER PLAY FOR LIFE

It's said that these wise words belong to Calvin Coolidge, thirtieth president of the United States. It's tough to shut up and listen. It's even tougher to do it without being smug and judgmental. That's why Power Players are big fans of the thing they call 'active listening'. They listen closely, they are completely present when they listen and the person they are listening to feels that every single word is being absorbed. Listening well is the most compassionate thing a Power Player can do. So few of us can listen well and without motive or agenda.

▶ THE STORY

I watched a Power Player work a party where all she did was listen the whole night. She asked every person she spoke to about their story and got them talking. When she left the party there wasn't a single person who really knew her story because she made it her business to engage other people and listen intently to whatever it was they needed and wanted to share. Five hours of listening to people—and the funny thing was that her life was for sure the most interesting in the room. Now that's real power.

⬆ CREATE A VACUUM

POWER PLAY FOR WORK

Power Players know that when you create a vacuum in your world, it has to get filled with the very thing that's missing. Creating a vacuum is a hidden-gem Power Play that the most experienced Players make. It is an act of courage and an act of faith, and if you want people to step up, create a vacuum. People usually do.

▶ THE STORY

The best example I have is from a power-playing CEO who was struggling to infuse some energy and flair into his management team. Rather than gently cajole his marginally talented head of strategy to do better and be better, he fired his lazy arse and created a vacuum. As they were without a strategy person, others in the management team had to step up to fill the vacuum and, in the process, one of the more junior members of the management team started to show her considerable talents, was given more room to run and became perhaps the best head of strategy the company has ever seen.

↑ WHEN YOU'RE ON A ROLL, ROLL!

POWER PLAY FOR WORK

Power Players know when to roll with it. Serendipity in business doesn't happen all that often, and sometimes it happens at the least opportune times. Just because it doesn't fit the timing plan, Power Players don't ignore this good fortune. So when they find themselves on a roll, they roll with it. They change timing plans and take advantage of karma, luck or whatever you want to call it. They let go of their preconceived ideas and best-laid plans. They roll with it and they improvise. Power Players see it as a liberating experience, and they relish the chance to work without a script and without a safety net. Next time you're on a roll, deviate from the plan and see where it takes you. I'm betting money it will be to a better destination than the one you first planned.

▶ THE STORY

I was meeting a colleague who was going to join a project I was part of too. Before I got to the restaurant where we were having a quick bite, I'd made the decision to wrap it up quickly; I didn't know her and she didn't know me. But as we got talking, I realised how very special she was and together we started brainstorming some ideas. At the time I remember thinking how I'd almost written off the meeting before it began and how we now found ourselves on this unbelievable creative bent. Never miss an opportunity to roll with it when you're on a roll.

YOU'RE NOT GOD

POWER PLAY FOR LIFE

Power Players don't fall into the trap of the God complex. They aren't superhuman, they can't fix everything, and they know this from the start. But this doesn't mean that you shouldn't have a shot at making a big play even if it will never happen. Why? There's a line I love from a *West Wing* episode and it goes something like this: 'You can't fix everything but I do like watching you try.' It's the trying part that is especially wonderful about Power Players. The crème de la crème Players know the difference between trying to fix an impossible problem and walking around with a God complex. One is good and noble, the other is an unmistakable characteristic of douche-baggery. You're not God so don't even try to be.

▸ THE STORY

About a hundred, but none that I can share.

FORGIVE

POWER PLAY FOR LIFE

Most of us think we can forgive but many of us do no such thing. It takes great compassion to forgive, especially when the transgression is pretty bad. Power Players make an honest choice. First they decide if they can forgive. If they can't, they don't, and they do what they can to have little to do with that person ever again. If they can forgive, they do it, and then they move on. They never dredge up the past and, more importantly, they never use it as ammunition. But the most important part of this whole story (and Power Players do this very well) is facing the reality of what forgiveness means: digging deep for the compassion most of us hope will be felt by someone else if we are the ones who screw up. And if you have chosen not to forgive, it also means that you judge the transgression as something you would never do—and that's a big call to make.

▶ THE STORY

There's no story I can tell you that will convince you to forgive. A forgiving heart is a good thing to nurture. Nurture it every chance you get. To err is human. To forgive really is divine.

TELL A GREAT STORY

POWER PLAY FOR EVERY SINGLE DAY

Power Players collect great stories as they move through their lives and remember them to use at just the right time. Become a great storyteller. Why? Because a great story is the exclamation mark in life. Stories animate and captivate the imagination, and my favourite Power Players tell some of the best stories I've heard. Get comfortable sharing stories, telling stories, and working out what makes for a good story in the first place. This is the most important part. Listen closely to the people who are great storytellers; see how they use words to illuminate and illustrate. It's a great talent to acquire. So get cracking on collecting those stories and telling them to your audience with great energy and passion.

▶ THE STORY

My brother tells some of the best stories in the world. They often centre on some humiliating (but funny) event that he had either played a role in or witnessed. He has a great way of capturing the absurdity of people when they feel they have been wronged or are liquored up. The stories are always sweet or wry, never cruel or taunting, so you see the sweetness or vulnerability of human beings. He never offends anybody and always embellishes the human part, which makes the listener feel the 'there but for the grace of God go I' aspect.

ASK A GREAT QUESTION

POWER PLAY FOR WORK

Power players are fantastic at asking the killer question. In business, this is one of the smartest things anyone can do because smart questions tell everyone in the room that the Power Player has a keen understanding of what's important and where things are going. Moreover, a great question makes for a much more interesting and thoughtful response. How many times in your life has someone asked you a really great question? One that stops you in your tracks and makes you rethink everything. Yeah, not that often. It's the same for clients and colleagues. Keep asking great questions because it will stretch your mind and your perspective.

▸ THE STORY

This story isn't about business at all. It's about a friend of mine who seemed loaded up with family responsibilities. Whenever I asked him how he was doing, he never talked about himself: he talked about his father, his brother, his work, and then all the things on his to-do list. He never seemed particularly happy or joyful. I figured out pretty quickly that his role in the family was to take care of everybody else. At one point I turned to him and asked, 'And who takes care of you?' The question stopped him in his tracks. He recently told me that question changed him enough to start rethinking everything about his life. One question.

STAND UP FOR SOMEONE

POWER PLAY FOR LIFE

And not just on a bus. Power Players take the high road when someone has been blindsided or treated unfairly. That line about all evil needing to succeed is for good men to stand by and do nothing comes to mind. Don't be complicit in bad behaviour. When someone has been wronged, don't stand by idly and leave them hanging. Jump in and do the right thing. You don't have to know the person to help.

▸ THE STORY

A friend of mine once jumped into the middle of a group of thugs harassing a girl. He just happened to be walking by and couldn't stand the thought of leaving the girl to contend with a group of drunken louts. Power Players will always do the right thing and stand up for someone who needs support. No matter how it turns out—my friend took a few hits from the drunken idiots—stand up and be counted. That's the job of a Power Player.

YOU'RE NOT THE STORY

POWER PLAY FOR LIFE

Power Players keep their eyes squarely on the story. They don't look for ways to insert themselves into the mix. We all come across those people who can always make themselves the star of the story. Power Players never pull this lame trick. If it's not about you, don't try to pretend it is. Power Players know when to keep the spotlight off them and on the place (or person) it actually belongs. This is one of those invaluable lessons that you should learn as quickly as you can because it's hard to come back from looking like a spotlight-stealing drama queen. No one likes a pretend superstar. It lacks class and erodes credibility as well.

▶ THE STORY

Someone I absolutely do not like always manages to make himself the star of the show. At a surprise birthday party, he turned up late (just after the birthday girl arrived and as we all yelled 'surprise') and stole the limelight. He'd had some exciting work news that he immediately had to tell everyone. He was so self-absorbed that the reason for the evening was almost forgotten. When the birthday cake came out (with candles) for the birthday girl, he blew the candles out with her. Talk about muscling in on someone else's story! Awful stuff.

NEVER OFFEND

POWER PLAY FOR LIFE

Power Players know how to dissent and disagree without offending, and this is harder to do than one would think. It means choosing your words very carefully and more or less rehearsing your dissent in your head before blurting it out loud. Disagreement delivered in a good way can actually be charming, believe it or not. There's no need to offend. It's short-sighted and evidence of lazy thinking. Choosing your words carefully means people will see your feedback as justified and they won't be sidetracked by the delivery. Start practising now.

▶ THE STORY

Here's one I heard recently and it knocked my socks off: 'You are extraordinarily good at your job and you're a joy to work with, but this idea of yours is not at all good. In fact, it's a stinker. I disagree with you that we can't find a better idea. You have before and you will again.' It was a direct torpedoing of an idea without ever offending. The person on the receiving end of this speech said this in return: 'It didn't feel like a very good idea but everyone else was telling me it would work. You're the first person who gave it to me straight. Thanks for telling me the truth.' The truth, told well, rarely offends.

➊ DON'T HECKLE

POWER PLAY FOR LIFE

There's a reason why comedians hate hecklers: it's cruel and dumb and shows an inferior mind. There's a big difference between some gentle good-natured teasing and plain old heckling. Don't do it. It's demeaning and it's usually symptomatic of a lot of passive aggressive crap. It's also self-seeking, and Power Players don't seek attention like children; attention comes to them because they have something worth saying. Resist that terrible urge we all sometimes have to heckle and take a lead from Power Players who feel a bitchy comment rising up inside them. Instead of voicing it, they drink from a glass of water or doodle something on their notepad until cooler heads prevail. Remember this: it's always easy to heckle from the cheap seats. You'll regret it when you do, so don't, and every Power Player worth their salt will tell you exactly the same thing.

► THE STORY

No story. Just don't do it.

RESPECT YOURSELF

POWER PLAY FOR LIFE

In a desperate bid to get stuff done, we all trade in our self-respect from time to time. It's easy to do and hard to claw back, so think long and hard about the price you pay for keeping somebody else happy. You can survive humiliation. You can survive failure. You can survive ridicule. But it's much harder to survive the obliteration of your self-respect. Nothing is worth it if it makes you feel cheap and easy. Loss of self-respect comes from knowing what you should do and choosing not to do it. It's hard to look at yourself in the mirror when you don't like what you see. Learn to grow a healthy measure of self-respect: it will save your bacon more times than you can count.

▶ THE STORY

My business partner and I had a meeting with a guy who was trying to roadblock a project, despite his client already agreeing to being financially involved. Seeing this guy was a courtesy, but he hated that we had a direct relationship with his client. We, on the other hand, didn't mind having to bring him into the picture given he'd need to be involved. Arriving at his office for our meeting, he kept us waiting in the lobby for twenty-nine minutes; we could see him through the glass of his corner office sitting at his desk. As he finally got up from his chair, my partner turned to me and said, 'We're out of here.' And we left. When his client later found out what had happened he was taken off the project and soon after he was fired. We'd been courteous, professional and patient, but we drew the line at being treated so disdainfully. We also should have left at least nine minutes earlier.

⬆ KNOW WHAT SUCCESS REALLY COSTS YOU

POWER PLAY FOR WORK

Power Players have an uncanny understanding of the price of success. If it costs you your dignity or your friends or your relationship, then it's too high a price. Success is one of those funny words that sounds great in theory but in practice is something else altogether. Know what you're willing to trade or give up in return for success—most of us don't until it's too late. Power Players take a good, long look at what success will look like after the fact. Will they be able to live with the trade-offs they've made? Make sure you ask yourself these questions before you go chasing your success story.

▶ THE STORY

In order to get a project off the ground, I had to spend an interminable amount of time with a man I really do not like. Every time I had to meet with him I started to feel sick in the stomach. It started to affect everything else in my orbit but I had convinced myself that without him I couldn't get this project off the ground, which was probably true. I gritted my teeth and held on for six months until I faked a reason not to meet with him. Now I was lying too. The next day I pulled the pin on the project and immediately started to feel better. The project would have been a great success but the price to pay was too high.

GRATITUDE: DON'T LOSE IT

POWER PLAY FOR LIFE

It may be a little saccharine but some of the most interesting Power Players keep a gratitude diary. It's a daily reminder of all the good stuff. They write down one thing a day for which they should be grateful. Why? When success becomes a way of life, it's easy to forget just how good you've got it. That's why Power Players don't tempt fate by becoming complacent (and arrogant) about good fortune. Sure, Power Players make their own luck, but they also know that if they forget to acknowledge how much they've got, it can quickly go away. Be grateful. Do it every day. Don't get lazy about seeing all the good things in your life because Power Players never do.

▶ THE STORY

My very good friend started to get blasé and cynical about his unbelievable success. Soon things started to go wrong—nothing big, just small things here and there. He started to get a little testy with people around him and soon bigger things started to go wrong. One night after a particularly bad day at the office he got home and sat quietly wondering why things were starting to feel off. He emailed a friend who is a Buddhist monk and the monk replied with two words: 'Show gratitude.' My friend went out and purchased a beautiful leather-bound book and started his gratitude diary. Every night before he puts his head down on his pillow he now writes one thing in his diary for which he should be grateful. The bad luck went away. Could be coincidence, probably is. But having gratitude never hurt anyone.

GIVE AN AWESOME PEP TALK

POWER PLAY FOR WORK

Power Players can give a pep talk as good as the one in *Braveheart*. When Mel Gibson's William Wallace bellows, 'They may take our lives but they will never take our freedom,' you want to jump to your feet and applaud. It's the type of oratory that makes you want to be better and do better, courageous and herculean. Power Players can give a Hollywood-sized pep talk, the type that makes its audience ignore fear, exhaustion, doubt and self-loathing. Power Players know that a great pep talk contains three ingredients: heart, encouragement and truth. Pep talks are required at the lowest possible moments, right when everyone wants to lie down and die. Learn how to give an awesome pep talk. It's mandatory for every aspiring Player.

▶ THE STORY

A little design business had lost its confidence and its key team was about to go into a pitch meeting to hopefully win some new business. The CEO sensed a feeling of fear and dread had come over the team (they'd lost a few pitches in a row) and she said this: 'We are winners, all of us. We each left our previous businesses to start our own and that takes real courage. We're talented, we're visionary and, to top it all, we're good people too. We're the people that other people want to talk to at a party, so for Christ's sake let's get in there and show them what we've got!' Immediately the mood changed, shoulders were broader, faces were happy and gaits were confident. They won the business.

KNOW THERE'S NO NORMAL

POWER PLAY FOR LIFE

One of the absolute best things about Power Players is that they don't fall into the trap of believing there's such a thing as normal. What's normal? Who's normal? And what's so great about normal anyway? A person can spend years worrying about being normal, all the while losing sight of the very character traits that make them special. Normal can also be unimaginative, boringly predictable and completely and totally overrated, so take a lead from your power-playing brethren and don't get caught up in doing what's normal if it doesn't feel right for you. And by the way, are all those 'normal' people happier than the rest of us? There's no evidence to suggest this so relax. You're as normal (or abnormal) as everybody else.

▶ THE STORY

I'm irregular. I suspect a lot of other people are irregular too. It took me a long time to recognise that I make my money by being irregular. I attract other irregular people and, when I look back at every single opportunity that has come my way, they've all been because I'm irregular. If you flip this another way, irregular means you're a little bit special. Run with it, because goodness knows there is far too much regular in the world. It's the originals who tend to get great jobs, live great lives and have a lot more fun than everyone else.

SET THE TONE

POWER PLAY FOR LIFE

Power Players take the lead when it comes to setting the tone. That's a pretty hard thing to do when you're having a shitty day, but Power Players know that you never get a second chance to make a first impression. Power Players also know that setting the right tone means you have to be completely and totally in the moment, and this is incredibly hard to do. If you manage to do it, you deserve the Power Player badge. Set the tone and see what happens when the room is inspired by great energy, rather than the kind that makes you go looking for the nearest trapdoor.

▶ THE STORY

I hosted a fancy work dinner for a team of colleagues. Everyone was pretty nervous. I poured myself a glass of wine and told the table that I thought a glass or two of wine would make the evening much more bearable. There were laughs and everyone immediately relaxed—and knew it was okay to relax!

ASK FOR WISDOM FROM THE RIGHT PEOPLE

POWER PLAY FOR LIFE

Wisdom is a great word that carries great power, and Power Players seek the wisest of counsel when they need it most. Don't fall for the bum steer: when you're seeking advice, make sure you go to the smartest and wisest people you know. Half the trick is working out which people to approach, and here are three ways that Power Players do it: first, they find the people whose counsel comes without some self-serving payoff; second, they find someone who can actually keep a secret; and third, they seek out people who lean naturally toward tolerance rather than judgment. Power Players ask for wise counsel when they need it most. Find some of these wise counsellors too and you'll be imitating one of the best Power Player moves there is.

► THE STORY

There's really only one person to whom I turn when I need solid, won't-let-me-down, need-to-hear-it wisdom. And he knows who he is. He makes me do three things: he gets me to tell the story slowly, he asks me why I think I'm really stumped, and he gets me to tell him what would happen if I did the opposite of what I'm thinking of doing and what would happen if I did what I'm thinking of doing. At no time does he pass judgment or push me into a corner. When you find the right person, hold on tight.

DON'T PRESUME WHAT'S IMPORTANT TO ANOTHER

POWER PLAY FOR LIFE

Power Players don't presume to know what goes on inside somebody else's head. If something matters to you, it doesn't automatically mean everybody else should care too. Power Players get to know over time what matters to the people in their circle. It's easy to think you know someone well because you spend a good deal of time with them but Power Players are careful not to fall into this trap. It takes a really long time to know what makes someone tick and Power Players are great at building relationships slowly. The flipside of this is that when you do get (a little bit) inside someone's head, it's fantastic knowing what they rate as important. And they'll be forever grateful that you never presumed to 'know' them.

▶ THE STORY

There's a guy who used to work for me who really needed me to comment on any emails or text messages he sent me, even to just acknowledge that I'd received them. If I didn't respond it would really bother him. It wouldn't have bothered me if someone hadn't responded to mine and I could never understand why he saw it as a sign of rejection or whatever, but once I worked this out I always made sure that I responded to each and every email. It made such a difference to his psyche and I was happy to oblige. Find out what matters and make it matter to you too.

HIRE TALENTED ENEMIES

POWER PLAY FOR WORK

This play is hard to do, which is why only the most secure Power Players do it. Power Players love smart people who disagree with them. This is why they hire talented enemies. Enemies might be too strong a word: more like people who have the guts to hold an opinion contrary to their own. It's hard to listen to someone argue a case that results in their being right and your being wrong. Power Players know that the most talented people sometimes even work for the competition. It takes real class to go after someone you know is probably smarter and has more natural talent than you. When you've mastered the art of hiring talented enemies, you know you've made it to the Power Player premier league.

▶ THE STORY

The chairman and CEO of an ad agency told me a story about continually losing pitches to a guy who was the managing director in another ad agency. He'd lost five pitches in a row and enough was enough. He rang up the guy and asked if they could meet for a drink. The guy was understandably uneasy about the whole thing but agreed. At the bar, the guy was prepared for anything except what happened next. The chairman and CEO offered this guy the top job (*his* job, the CEO gig), saying he'd stay on in the chairman role. He doubled his salary on the spot and told him that together they would be an unbeatable force. The guy jumped ship and together they won an unprecedented twelve pitches in a row. Talk about impressive.

'THE REALLY GREAT MAKE YOU FEEL THAT YOU, TOO, CAN BECOME GREAT'

POWER PLAY FOR WORK

Mark Twain said this and he really knew what he was talking about. Power Players make those around them feel like greatness is completely part of their modus operandi. For Power Players, greatness isn't about showing off their greatness but about bringing out the courage that makes each of us feel we too can reach for the great stuff. A rare few people we come into contact with bring out the best version of ourselves, the one that makes us feel we can fulfil all the crazy dreams we carry around in our heads. If you want to be a really top Power Player, make others feel that they have the great gene too.

► THE STORY

My dad had this way of making you feel like you could do anything. When he walked into a room the entire temperature would change. People would stand up straight, fix their hair, smile and become the best version of themselves. He saw the potential in people, their talents and all their possibilities. He found ways to talk to them that inspired them and made them feel like the risk was worth it. He located their greatness switch and turned it on. He would ask them what they loved doing and urge them to find a way to do it every day. He used to say, 'Find out what you love and do it on purpose every day.' Now that's great.

WHEN YOU OVERTHINK, STOP THINKING

POWER PLAY FOR LIFE

I heard this from a power-playing ballet dancer. He told me that the key to being a great dancer is to stay away from the trapdoor of overthinking. Apparently when great dancers start to overthink the pirouette or that grand finale move, they flub it. It's the same in business. Overthinking a decision ends up like overchurned cream: it becomes something else entirely—butter. The absolute second you start fixating and churning on a problem, stop thinking altogether. Change the scenery, change the topic and change the company you are keeping. Nine times out of ten overthinking is actually counterproductive to whatever problem you are trying to solve. And if you follow this advice, there's a good chance that when you wake up the next morning, the solution to your quandary will have presented itself without any interference whatsoever.

▶ THE STORY

No story: just stop!

'TO BE SIMPLE IS TO BE GREAT'

POWER PLAY FOR WORK

Ralph Waldo Emerson, who wrote these seven words, stated what is absolutely true. So much of our lives are deliberately wrapped up in complexity. We love to add layers and layers of confusion and intrigue when none is required. Power Players love to pare it back. They don't need fancy words and impressive strategies and convoluted theories to show how smart they are. They worked out long ago that true greatness is to be found in cutting through the pretence and hyperbole. To be clear and simple in thought and deed, to give direct and uncomplicated instructions, to take the shortest route to the finish line, to use five words when everyone else uses fifty: these are all things that make for a great Power Player.

▶ THE STORY

The best boss I ever had could take the most complex, convoluted plans and turn them into simple English. Simple, but not simplistic. He never buried the headline and he explained things in a way that a four-year-old could understand, but never in a way that was condescending or patronising. He could distil it all in an incredibly entertaining way as well. Where others dedicated energy to making it complex and elaborate, he would pause before speaking, giving him enough time to make it crystal and clean. Even his word selection was straightforward: he would use ten where others would use fifty. Simple is elegant. Simple is beautiful. And the great minds know it.

STEP UP OR STEP OFF

POWER PLAY FOR WORK

Power Players have a wonderful way of simplifying leadership in five simple words: step up or step off. Power Players know that the only way to be a leader is to lead, and this means stepping up when the situation requires it and taking the reins. If stepping up isn't required, Power Players know the only thing left is to step off. This is a total Power Player characteristic: become a strong and decisive leader or step to one side and let someone else lead. When it comes to leadership, there is no in-between. You can't lead 'just a little bit' and Power Players know this better than anyone. If you decide to step up, do it well, do it thoroughly and do it wholeheartedly. When it comes to leadership, pick a side, in or out. And remember these five magic words: step up or step off.

▶ THE STORY

A wonderful woman I know recruits and trains staff for a sales team. She is the designated leader so she leads. She is a fan of a particular style of selling and, given she is a part-owner of the business, has decided that this will be the way her staff should be trained. She isn't into collaboration or letting individuals decide how they'd like to sell. It's her way or no way at all. I hugely admire her style: she has stepped up and claimed leadership wholeheartedly because she has a lot of evidence proving that her way is very effective. She is decisive, strong and exactly what a leader should be in her industry.

‘GREAT HOPES MAKE GREAT MEN’

POWER PLAY FOR LIFE

Thomas Fuller, a prolific English author from the seventeenth century, was a big fan of hope and he wrote this line. Power Players always have hope, especially in terrible times when all they want to do is jackknife off a balcony. Why? Because this is when hope is most needed. Hope is a little bit like faith: most of the time there is absolutely no reason to have hope, and most regular people need the data and evidence in order to be hopeful. Having hope is required in order to be powerful. It means you've got some extra goodwill on your side, and just having that additional momentum is sometimes enough to have things go your way. It's also quite a beautiful quality because it flies in the face of cynicism and despair. Hope is the line between powerless and powerful. Have some—you might find you like it.

▶ THE STORY

A young trader I met named Mitchell set me straight about love. He told me that I should never rule out the possibility of love. He said that he was a hopeless romantic; I said I was just hopeless. He told me to stop with the cynicism: he wasn't buying it and hope made living worthwhile. He told me that when it comes to love there is always hope, and that's what made life fun. He told me that deep down he knew I was a romantic and that I had hope. I knew him for an hour and he opened my eyes to how great hopes can make you great.

BAD EXCUSES ARE WORSE THAN NONE

POWER PLAY FOR LIFE

This sentiment can be attributed to the seventeenth-century English author Thomas Fuller, but it rings true today too. Power Players have more self-respect than to serve up a lame excuse. If you're late for work, simply apologise—using a lame excuse is as bad as it is unimaginative. Excuses in general are lowbrow and just ways to avoid taking responsibility for the problem you've created. Power Players know what most of us don't: excuses usually prolong the problem. An apology for screwing up is the much more noble route. Excuses are for the weak and cowardly. Take a big lesson from Power Players: don't get into the messy habit of resorting to a lame excuse. Tell the truth. Give no excuse. Accept the consequences of your actions. Apologise. If you make a mistake, take your medicine and wait for it to wash over.

▶ THE STORY

When my friend had a meltdown about a clothing malfunction before we were supposed to head off to a day out with friends, it made me nuts. I think it was simply an excuse not to go, and if so, my friend should have just said so. Instead I had to call the host to say that we were not going to be joining her for lunch. Humiliating. Don't make lame excuses. Tell the truth.

➊ WISDOM IS KNOWING WHAT TO OVERLOOK

POWER PLAY FOR LIFE

We all know that wisdom is a big (and loaded) word. But the part that most of us don't know is that wisdom knows what to overlook. Not every event or problem needs to be analysed. Not every problem needs to be solved. Not every problem needs to be put under a bright light and interrogated. It's like listening to somebody tell a really bad joke and jumping right over it when nobody laughs—best to act like it never happened. Most of us can't let anything go: we need to chew it over until it's been examined from every angle. Power Players know exactly what to overlook because they know what happens if they investigate something that needs to be left alone: chaos. Get wise on what to overlook.

▸ THE STORY

I watched my friend say something awful to another friend in the ballpark of 'You've never really had a fantastic career because you've just had a job'. The offender didn't mean to say it—she'd had a bad day and it simply flew out of her mouth. The friend to whom she'd said it skipped right over it, hugged her and never raised it again. She did exactly what she was supposed to do: she overlooked it.

REVENGE IS THE POISON WE END UP SWALLOWING OURSELVES

POWER PLAY FOR LIFE

Everyone has a revenge fantasy. I've had a million. But Power Players know that revenge is the poison we end up swallowing ourselves. Nothing good comes from flexing your angry and vindictive talents. All it does is make you look small and pathetic. The best revenge is forgiving your enemies; nothing else annoys them nearly as much. The other truth Power Players know is that revenge ages you. It's full of bitterness and rancour, and these bad attributes seep into your soul. They make you lose your sense of humour. They make you focus on what you've lost rather than on what you have. And the worst thing about revenge is that showing your enemy how much they've rattled you lets them win. Ignore them. It's the only classy way to go.

► THE STORY

A woman who'd love to see me sweat pushes me to the end of my revenge cliff. It's taken me years but now I simply forgive every single one of her cruel jibes and mean comments. She's the classic frenemy and the love I heap on her makes her crazy and keeps me sane.

⬆ TOUGH TIMES DON'T LAST: TOUGH PEOPLE DO

POWER PLAY FOR WORK

Power Players always reach for this when it all goes south. You haven't lived if you haven't had some very tough times, but the beauty of tough times is that they don't last forever. On the other hand, tough people do. Power Players are just tough enough to survive whatever thunderstorm is coming their way, but not so tough that they become unfeeling and cruel. Tough Power Players still go home and cry when it's awful—then get a good night's sleep and face the tough stuff again the next day. Learn to toughen up in the same way that Power Players do. It will keep you alive during tough times but still allow you to feel genuinely alive when the good times start to roll.

▶ THE STORY

My sister has an internal fortitude that is extraordinary, yet she is sweet and gentle and kind, tough without the hard, which is really hard to do. When she is having a particularly tough day, she digs in and faces it head on and gets it sorted. A manufacturer for her business who wasn't cutting the mustard needed to be read the riot act. She was firm and sorted him out, and then she resumed being her sweet, wonderful self. Hard to do without becoming gristle.

↑ IF A SIX-YEAR-OLD DOESN'T GET IT . . .

POWER PLAY FOR WORK

No one else will either. If you've got a six-year-old handy, try out your thinking on them. If they don't get it, then maybe you should start again. Power Players road-test their ideas on people who have no background in what they're working on. They don't cut corners on this one; it's cheating when you share your ideas with people who are already in the inner circle. Go way, way outside the circle and turn to fresh eyes and a fresh head. The six-year-old example might be a little extreme in some cases, but you know what I mean. The best Power Players I know do in fact use kids as a sounding board, probably because kids have no filter and they ask questions when they don't understand something. If a six-year-old doesn't get it, maybe a sixty-year-old won't either.

► THE STORY

My favourite CEO used to go to our work canteen and talk to the people in the kitchen. He'd share an idea with them and get them to react honestly. Once he went in there and talked about a new product we were developing for a major breakfast food company and they tore that idea to shreds. They said it made no sense, didn't really answer a need and they couldn't quite get it. Then they helped him come up with something better.

AFTERWORD

If this book proves anything, it's that there are plenty of examples out there of good power. The kind of power that is noble and pure and decent.

This gives me great hope for a future filled with people who, once they've achieved great power, use it for good.

Corny? Maybe.

But I believe the world can do with as much benevolent power as it can find.

For how much better is the world with people in it like Bill Gates; people who choose to give their money away?

If there were a million powerful people with the greater good in mind, and then two million and then three million and then even more, we could probably solve many of the ills and injustices of our society.

What would happen if every one of the world's citizens reached for good before evil? Or reached for kindness over cruelty? Or love over hate? The world would become a place we'd probably not recognise.

Next time you find yourself with power in your hands, no matter how big or small, try to let it be the good kind.

ACKNOWLEDGEMENTS

There are some very special people I'd like to acknowledge.

Eric Beecher, Chairman of Private Media. If it were not for Eric, this book would never have been written. Eric is never bigger than the game and treats the kid starting out in exactly the same way as he does the heavy-hitters in media, business and politics. It's really something to watch.

A man whom my late father would have liked very much: Michael Connaghan, Chief Executive Officer of the STW Group. Mike wears his power lightly and brings out the very best in people, myself included. This is hard to do and a gift all too rare.

And finally to my sister Anna and my brother Danny: the greatest relationships I've ever had in my life are with you guys. I've learnt more from you about the good kind of power than from anyone. In the lottery of siblings, I hit the jackpot.

THEMATIC INDEX

Power Play for every situation

Power Play for everywhere

Power Play for everywhere, but especially at work

Power Play for life

Power Play for work and play and in every single way

Power Play for work and relationships

Power Play for work, but use it at play too

Power Play for work (but more useful at play)

JAICO PUBLISHING HOUSE

Elevate Your Life. Transform Your World.

ESTABLISHED IN 1946, Jaico Publishing House is home to world-transforming authors such as Sri Sri Paramahansa Yogananda, Osho, The Dalai Lama, Sri Sri Ravi Shankar, Sadhguru, Robin Sharma, Deepak Chopra, Jack Canfield, Eknath Easwaran, Devdutt Pattanaik, Khushwant Singh, John Maxwell, Brian Tracy and Stephen Hawking.

Our late founder Mr. Jaman Shah first established Jaico as a book distribution company. Sensing that independence was around the corner, he aptly named his company Jaico ('Jai' means victory in Hindi). In order to service the significant demand for affordable books in a developing nation, Mr. Shah initiated Jaico's own publications. Jaico was India's first publisher of paperback books in the English language.

While self-help, religion and philosophy, mind/body/spirit, and business titles form the cornerstone of our non-fiction list, we publish an exciting range of travel, current affairs, biography, and popular science books as well. Our renewed focus on popular fiction is evident in our new titles by a host of fresh young talent from India and abroad. Jaico's recently established Translations Division translates selected English content into nine regional languages.

Jaico's Higher Education Division (HED) is recognized for its student-friendly textbooks in Business Management and Engineering which are in use countrywide.

In addition to being a publisher and distributor of its own titles, Jaico is a major national distributor of books of leading international and Indian publishers. With its headquarters in Mumbai, Jaico has branches and sales offices in Ahmedabad, Bangalore, Bhopal, Bhubaneswar, Chennai, Delhi, Hyderabad, Kolkata and Lucknow.

SINCE 1946